ISBN 978-0-9950756-1-0

Title: Eyes to See: Reflecting God's Love To A World In Need
Format: Paperback

© 2017 by Compassion Canada

Published by Compassion Canada,
985 Adelaide St. S,
London, ON,
N6E 4A3

Cataloguing data available from Library and Archives Canada

Printed in Canada.

Endorsements

Good intentions to help the poor are not enough. As followers of Jesus and fellow neighbours with people suffering in poverty, we must have both a heart and a mind for the poor. *Eyes to See* helps us develop both. This book will challenge you not only to participate in God's work of reconciliation, but to open yourself to be transformed as well. *Eyes to See* brings some of the best Christian thinkers on the topics of poverty, justice and reconciliation. But more than just a topical exploration, you also get to meet people like Simon, Michelle, and Anna and learn from their experiences overcoming obstacles and finding hope.

– Russ Debenport
Vice President of Programs, The Chalmers Center

Eyes to See is designed for those who want to understand why God cares so much for those in poverty and facing injustice and are prepared to learn how loving and serving the poor is an essential aspect of becoming a follower of Christ. Grounded in the sweep of Scripture from Genesis to Revelation, and full of practical ways to respond locally and globally, *Eyes to See* will equip its users to join Jesus today in a journey of restoration that will bring hope to many in our broken and violent world.

– Ed Wilson
Executive Director, International Justice Mission Canada

One of the first names of God in scripture is "the God who sees me." It is a powerful revelation indeed. The scriptures suggest that salvation involves repentance and repentance literally means to change our perception. *Eyes to See* offers us a chance to explore God and change the way we see the world. This is how salvation comes to earth! *Eyes to See* offers us an encounter with the God who sees us. It is a world changing perspective that is deeply needed in our current culture.

– Danielle Strickland
Social Justice Secretary, The Salvation Army

Compassion is the real deal. Having been on several trips with Compassion, I've seen first-hand the incredible impact their work has on children, families, and communities. Best of all, it's administered effectively through the local church—an approach that truly advances the Kingdom. This study will open your eyes, and your heart, to the role of the Church in caring for those in need.

– Carey Nieuwhof
Founding and Teaching Pastor, Connexus Church in Barrie, ON

For too long our conversation about poverty has been limited by stereotypes and myths that have hindered our response to God's call for justice. *Eyes to See* gives us a new language and perspective to understand poverty differently and opens up new ways for a faithful response. This is a powerful resource that will empower congregations to move beyond charity and creatively imagine more effective actions that embody God's vision of shalom.

– Derek Cook
Director of the Canadian Poverty Institute, Ambrose University

What a brilliant resource to help give us eyes to see from God's perspective what we often can't see or won't see because we feel overwhelmed with the need around us, or are simply distracted with what is happening in our own immediate world. *Eyes to See* gives us a unique view and a shares how we can practically bring the love of Jesus into a hurting and dying world. It brings a message of hope and solution and invites us to open our hearts and our hands to make a difference in the life of one person at a time. I truly appreciate the vibrant message of faith, hope and love that is woven into every chapter of this beautiful book.

– Helen Burns
Host, Hillsong Channel and Pastor, Relate Church in Surrey, BC

Nothing has been used of God in our family's heart like Compassion. And nothing is more important than eyes to see. "Looking comes first," wrote C.S. Lewis. First, the eyes. Change starts here. And *Eyes to See*—is an awakening that your soul, the church, and the world has been longing for. Not one of us can afford to look away.

– Ann Voskamp
Author of The New York Times bestsellers The Broken Way and One Thousand Gifts

I am always looking for resources that will serve the local church and believers well in understanding the complex dynamics at the intersection of faith and the world we live in. *Eyes to See* is such a resource. In a methodical and engaging way, individuals and small groups will find it easy to wrestle with the material and yet be challenged to make real changes that will shape and form them for a lifetime in tangible ways. Open your eyes and see what God can do with you when you get serious about knowing His will for your life and the lives of our neighbours in need across the world!

– Darren Roorda
Canadian Ministries Director, Christian Reformed Church in North America

Poverty is a complex issue. But, it's also simple. This resource helps us to understand many of its complexities, but also is built on a foundation that is Jesus. Without Jesus, we are all poor. We are excited to see this tool used to deepen your understanding and practice of how to bring Jesus and help to those in need.

– Rev. Wayne Smele
Executive Pastor of Global Mission, Centre Street Church in Calgary, AB

What would happen if you took six weeks out of your life to passionately seek God's perspective on our broken world? I think it would revolutionize you – and the world. *Eyes to See* guides us through this journey, helping us understand that poverty is not only external but that it lives within each one of us. I would challenge every person of faith to embark on this important journey.

– Cheryl Weber
Co-host, 100 Huntley Street

Compassion Canada has provided us with another tremendously valuable discipleship tool. *Eyes to See* is designed to ground us theologically, motivate us emotionally, and inspire us practically to engage more thoughtfully and substantively in issues of justice and poverty around the world. This resource will educate and ignite action that will both help us replicate the heart of God and meet needs in meaningful ways. Get it, read it, let it grip your heart and then live it!

– Dr. Michael B. Pawelke
President, Briercrest College & Seminary

Foreword

I first saw poverty in Haiti in 1984. I was three months into my role at Compassion and was sent to learn about our work in the field. I had travelled outside of Canada in the past, but this was different. I saw children gather water from a bat-infested cave, women carry pails on their heads for several kilometres each day and men bathe in ditches after a hard day's work. What I saw angered and overwhelmed me. I did not yet have the framework to properly understand and respond.

In more than three decades of working with children and families living in poverty, I have come to understand there is more to poverty than what meets the eye. So often poverty is reduced to mere material concerns and is depicted with a sense of hopelessness and despondency, or as something that happens "out there" to other people, rather than something that involves us personally. When that happens, we can easily become blind not just to the needs of people living in poverty, but also to our own impoverished, broken state.

But what if we saw poverty in a different light?

Eyes to See invites you to see again with new eyes: the eyes of Christ. Far from being blind to the needs of this world, He is the God who sees us; the Saviour who entered into our broken world to offer real hope. As you are challenged to deepen your relationship with Him, you will see how poverty uniquely affects us all, and how Jesus came to restore all that is broken.

Eyes to See draws on the collaborative knowledge and experiences of those at Compassion who have spent many years working in the field and alongside Canadian churches to release children from poverty in Jesus' name. Together, they provide deep insight and perspective on God's love for those living in poverty and evidence of His continuing reconciliation and healing in this world. This collective background makes *Eyes to See* a valuable resource for individuals and churches, providing them with a Biblical framework both to understand poverty and to respond to it.

Since that first trip to Haiti, I have travelled countless more times to the developing world. Each time, I meet people whose lives have been completely transformed by the gospel. These changed people have served their communities in whatever circumstance God has placed them, fueled by the love of Jesus and desire to make him known. I pray the same would be true for you. That throughout this journey you will not only be drawn closer to Christ, but in your everyday, ordinary life, will join him in his mission to bring His love and healing to the world.

– Barry Slauenwhite
President & CEO, Compassion Canada

Contents

Eyes to See

Reflecting God's Love
To A World In Need

When you were younger, did your mom ever tell you to finish your peas because there were starving children in the world? You knew her logic was suspect, even then. As far as you were concerned, they could have your peas. And how in the world would eating your peas help them anyway? Instead, you were left with both a vague feeling of guilt for what you had, and a feeling that you couldn't really do anything to help these hypothetical starving children anyhow.

Fast forward to today. Some of us still have those mingled feelings: a small, underlying guilt for what we have when faced with the needs in the world, coupled with a feeling of powerlessness in the enormity of these needs. Others of you might feel quite the opposite. You know that there are needs. You care. And you believe you can make a difference. But you also want to go deeper. You want to understand poverty in light of God's story. You don't want your response to simply be a knee-jerk reaction in the wrong direction, but you want to help in a godly and healthy way.

Maybe many of you feel a little afraid that if you go on this journey, your heart might break in pieces, and you won't be able to put it back together again.

No matter where you are coming from, we want you to know this: God has a beautiful plan for this broken world that He is unfolding even now, and He wants you to be a part of it. God reveals throughout the Bible His deep care for those in poverty and facing injustice.

When Jesus surveyed this world, He was filled with compassion: "When he saw the crowds, he had compassion on them, because they were harassed and helpless, like sheep without a shepherd," Matthew 9:36. As we walk with Christ, we ask God to transform us day by day, to be more like Him. And as we grow to be more like Christ, we will find our compassion for those around us begins to overflow, just as God's love overflows for us.

Our first step is to stop and ask God to give us eyes to see: To see the needs in our own backyard and around the world; to see what the roots of these problems are, rather than resorting to shallow or misguided solutions; to see how Canadians like us and God's people around the world are responding; and to see what our part could be.

That's what this journey will be all about. This book is divided into six weeks with five daily readings.

- The first week, we'll ask God to help us have eyes to see what the needs in Canada and in the world are, and what the ultimate solution to poverty really is.

- The second week, we'll ask God to help us see ourselves: what are the blind spots in our own lives that hold us back, and what is He calling us to?

- The third week, we'll ask God to help us better see Him, to understand His love, compassion, and plan of action for this world.

- The fourth week, we'll ask God to help us see others as He sees them, rather than through our own faulty lens of need.

- The fifth week, we'll ask God to help us see how we can be good stewards of the resources he has given us as we participate in His mission in the world.

- The sixth week, we'll end by asking God to help us see what practical steps we can take to be a reflection of His love in this broken world.

There are so many exciting stories of what is happening already. We invite you on this journey to see the world in a different way—the way God sees it: A world in which God wants to heal *you* in your own brokenness and bring healing to the many places where suffering lurks in this world; a world in which God wants to use both people living with economic wealth *and* people who are living in poverty to bring about change; a world in which God is calling His people everywhere to the urgent business of being bearers of His compassion, healing, and mercy.

***

This book is divided into 30 daily readings. At the end of each day's reading, you will find reflection questions to help you process what you're reading. There will also be an option for action. We encourage you to include these in your daily life as a way to help what God is teaching you to really sink in. Finally, there is a short prayer because all of this is really a dialogue with God, and none of us will see differently without God's intervention.

If you're interested in using this material with a small group, we recommend using it together with our film series *Eyes to See*—six videos that complement this six-week curriculum. You can download the small group leader guide and films at www.eyestosee.ca.

Ten Thousand Foot View

BIG PICTURE

Have you ever looked down on the area where you live from an airplane? You can see the lay of the land, where the rivers go, what is actually big and what is small. The shapes of things become clear. It's called taking the 10,000-foot view—getting the big picture.

That's what this week is all about: getting the big picture. God never intended poverty. After people disobeyed God, every aspect of life spun out of its intended orbit. This week, we'll go deeper in our understanding of poverty, exploring its spiritual roots and how that impacts all our relationships.

ADDITIONAL RESOURCES

- Armstrong, Aaron. *Awaiting a Savior: The Gospel, the New Creation and the End of Poverty.* Cruciform Press, 2011.

- Corbett, Steve, and Brian Fikkert. *When Helping Hurts: How to Alleviate Poverty Without Hurting the Poor... And Yourself.* Moody Publishers, 2014.

Choosing to See

"She gave this name to the Lord who spoke to her: 'You are the God who sees me,' for she said, 'I have now seen the One who sees me.'"

Genesis 16:13

"Humankind cannot bear very much reality."

– T.S. Eliot

Have you ever thought about which superpower you would most like? For many people, the ultimate dream would be the ability to fly. Others would like to teleport or travel through time. Still others would simply like the ability to sleep through the night or to get their kids to listen to them.

But some superpowers can backfire—like invisibility.

Sure, there are times when we would all love to move through the world without being noticed, but not all the time. And yet that is the daily reality for many people: they become part of the blur as we rush by. It's not possible for us to pay attention to every single person around us. Thankfully, God does see each person, each small celebration, each quiet tragedy.

In the next thirty days, we want to learn to see what God sees in the world around us. It's a bit like cleaning your glasses or taking a squeegee to your car windows.

At first, it can seem like people living in poverty or suffering injustice are somehow different from us. It's hard to really see them because we can't really relate; their experiences are so very different from our own. But the remarkable thing is that when we look closely, we see our commonality. We are far more alike than our outward circumstances might lead us to believe. We all have hopes. We all want the best for our families. We all laugh at funny things. We all cry when we are hurt.

So what might we *not* be seeing in the world around us?

Activist June Callwood called children, "Canada's invisible citizens," as she worked to address issues of child poverty and hunger in Canada. Children are the smallest among us, the least able to speak up for themselves, and the most vulnerable. It isn't just Canadian kids either. A few years ago, Compassion International President Emeritus, Wess Stafford, eagerly attended an international conference on mission and evangelism. He hoped to hear how others were bringing hope and help to children around the world. He began to keep a tally of how many times the speakers mentioned children. He learned that "children were not on the mind of any of these great leaders."

There are other people we don't see. The only time we hear about them is when they become part of a sad statistic: People who are homeless. Refugees who are stateless. People living in extreme poverty in faraway countries. Aboriginal people.

Terra was a First Nations woman living on the streets of Toronto when she was interviewed for a project about the invisibility of homeless people. She said, "It feels like no one cares about you, and they just disregard you."

At the Special Committee on Violence Against Indigenous Women in 2013, Connie Greyeyes of the Bigstone Cree Nation read a poem written by her niece, Helen Knott, called "Invisible":

Your eyes, they curve around me
I watch you try so hard to find your way past me.
Your sight is like rushing waters,
Moving beside me, behind me, pushing over me,
Indirectly consuming me...
You don't want to see me.
What's worse is that you have a choice whether or not you see me.
I become a casualty of your blindness...

As we begin this thirty-day journey, we want to admit that seeing is hard and that we often are overwhelmed by what we see. We turn on the news or go on social media only to shut it off again because the issues and images are too much. As the poet T.S. Eliot once said, "Humankind cannot bear very much reality." It's tempting to retreat into a Pinterest-perfect world and do our best to keep our own families safe and happy.

Other times, we are jarred awake by an image so heart-wrenching we cannot turn away. The Syrian refugee crisis had been going on for several years when the body of three-year-old Alan Kurdi washed up on the shores of Turkey—and suddenly people around the world were able to clearly see something that had previously been only abstract to them: that people like themselves were fleeing their homes. As Somali-British poet, Warsan Shire, wrote:

> "You have to understand,
> no one puts their children in a boat
> unless the water is safer than the land."

But there is another thing we sometimes fail to see: hope. God has not abandoned us in a world full of troubles. No one is invisible to God. He sees even those considered the most inconsequential to society. Genesis 16 tells us of Hagar, a rejected servant who was mistreated and fled into the desert. You couldn't get much lower on the social spectrum than Hagar. But she wasn't beneath God's notice. God knew of her misery and sent the angel of the Lord to help her. And Hagar "gave this name to the Lord who spoke to her: 'You are the God who sees me'" (Genesis 16:13). We serve a God who sees us. A God who sees all who are suffering in poverty and injustice. A God who longs to heal this broken world.

We can hope in Christ who tells us, "In this world you will have trouble. But take heart! I have overcome the world" (John 16:33). We can begin to see the world as God sees it because we know that He offers a real and tangible hope. As we embark on this journey, we ask God to help us have His eyes in this world that is thick with paradox: full of incredible beauty and love, and, at the same time, with brokenness, pain and poverty.

Reflection

 01   Who is usually invisible to you?

 02   When you actually see such people, how do you feel?

 03   What is the hope that enables you to look at reality?

Action

When you walk or drive down the street today, keep your eyes open for people who are usually invisible to you.

Prayer

God, It's not a stretch to say that we can only bear so much reality. Thank You for reminding us that You can handle all reality and that is exactly what you did in dying for all of us on the cross. Over the next six weeks, would You help me begin to see what You see? Would you help me to see through a lens of hope that You are already working in the darkest corners of the world? Thank You for seeing me where I am right now. Amen.

The Story of Poverty

"So God created mankind in his own image, in the image of God he created them; male and female he created them. God blessed them and said to them, 'Be fruitful and increase in number; fill the earth and subdue it. Rule over the fish in the sea and the birds in the sky and over every living creature that moves on the ground.'"

Genesis 1:27-28

"The original shalom vision was a cosmic vision of wholeness, harmony, unity, justice and love between God and humans, between man and woman, within each human person, and between humans and the rest of the created world. The scope of the fall was also cosmic, disrupting the relationships between God and humanity and the entire created order."

– Bethany Hoang and Kristen Johnson

It wasn't supposed to be this way. Poverty was never God's plan.

If we go back to the start of the book of Genesis and the story of Creation, we see that people were created in the image of God in a world that God declared "very good." When we read the first couple of chapters of Genesis, we see the initial relationship of Adam and Eve who felt no shame at their nakedness and who were intimately connected as "bone of my bone and flesh of my flesh." We see how Adam and Eve were given good work tending the Garden of Eden. We see how they had plenty to eat, and were enjoying the fruits of their work. We read about how they would walk with God in the garden in the cool of the day. It was a world in which poverty could not exist.

And then.

And then people did the one thing God had told them not to do. And what happened had a massive ripple effect. It didn't just damage the relationship with God, but it broke all the other relationships which had characterized the way God had designed people to live.

We were designed for relationships. God—who is relational in His very nature as Father, Son and Holy Spirit—made us to be like Him in that relational image. Even in the short version we get in Genesis, we can see that God intended us to have four fundamental relationships: with ourselves, God, others and creation. When those relationships are healthy and functioning, we are able to enjoy life as He intended it: free from poverty, oppression, injustice and brokenness.

But now, as Brian Fikkert and Steve Corbett point out in *When Helping Hurts*, every one of those relationships is broken. Adam and Eve's intimacy with God was replaced by fear. Within themselves, they now felt shame. The intimacy between Adam and Eve was now blocked by blame. Their once fulfilling work was now "painful toil."

Today, so many generations later, all of us still experience these same broken relationships. We no longer trust solely in God, so we believe we must fend for ourselves—leading to greed, hoarding and countless injustices. In our broken relationship with ourselves, our shame leads us to destructive behaviour to find belonging and acceptance. Our relationships with one another are plagued by sin that leads to poverty, war, abandonment and abuse. Disease, drought and natural disasters are constant reminders that our relationship with creation is broken; we no longer live in the safe and hospitable Garden of Eden.

None of these problems would have existed if people had chosen to stay in that unbroken relationship with God. This doesn't mean that each person's circumstances are a direct result of their poor choices, or that good choices will always lead to positive circumstances. Very often people's suffering or poverty is due to things such as unjust systems, corruption, disease, war and environmental degradation—all results of the Fall.

The Bible itself reveals various reasons for poverty. Injustice leads to poverty, as Proverbs 13:23 says, "A person's farm may produce much food, but injustice sweeps it all away" (NLT). Foolish choices can lead to poverty, as Proverbs 28:19 says, "Those who work their land will have abundant food, but those who chase fantasies will have their fill of poverty" (NIV). Social isolation can deepen poverty, as Proverbs 19:4 says: "Wealth attracts many friends, but even the closest friend of the poor deserts them." And, although there are often character attacks on those living in poverty, the Bible reveals that just as the poor can be both wise and foolish, so can the wealthy. As Proverbs 28:11 says, "The rich are wise in their own eyes, but one who is poor and discerning sees how deluded they are."

Regardless of the cause, we tend to think of poverty as an economic problem requiring an economic solution. We assume poverty only means a lack of things or money. But its roots go much deeper and further back. Bryant Myers, a leading Christian development thinker, puts it plainly: "Poverty is fundamentally relational and its cause is fundamentally spiritual." Our relationship with God was broken in the Fall. Our relationships with each other are broken. Our relationship with God's creation is broken. And even our relationship with ourselves is broken. Brokenness is the root of poverty.

Because these four relationships are the building blocks of all human activity, the ripples of the Fall can be seen in all of our systems, from economics, to politics and even to our churches.

Notice the words "us" and "our." When we think of poverty in terms of broken relationships, with its roots being spiritual, we stop thinking of the poor as "them." Instead, we begin to recognize that we are all poor in one way or another. Some of us experience deep financial poverty. Some of us experience deep relational poverty. Some of us struggle to find God. Others struggle with feelings of low self-worth or loneliness. Every human being from the wealthiest to the poorest experiences poverty because we don't experience these fundamental relationships in the way God intended.

In the 1970s, Tony Neeves made the decision to leave a promising job in advertising to become the communications director of a new non-profit in the UK, Tearfund. On one of his first visits to the developing world, he went to Guinea Bissau and witnessed the extreme poverty of the subsistence farmers. As he said goodbye to one of the villagers he had met, he told him he would pray for him because he was so poor. The villager said that he would pray for Neeves as well, saying, "as you are also so poor." Neeves was puzzled. He wasn't poor at all, so he asked the villager why he had said this.

The villager replied, "Oh, you are poor! You have God, and things that take your eyes off God. We have only God."

The story of poverty—as much as it might surprise us—is *our* story.

Reflection

 01 Do you agree with this definition of poverty? Why or why not?

02 What forms of poverty do you see in your own life?

03 How do you react to the idea that you are poor?

Action

Ask someone to pray for a need of yours regarding one of the four relationships you struggle most with.

Prayer

Lord, if I'm honest, I don't like the idea of admitting my own poverty. I feel a bit like Adam and Eve in the garden, trying to cover my nakedness and shame. But you know who I am. You know my needs, my poverty, as well as the ways in which I am wealthy. As I reflect about poverty, help me to accept the reality of brokenness in my own life, too. Amen.

DAY 3

The Reality of Poverty

"Cursed is the ground because of you; through painful toil you will eat food from it all the days of your life. It will produce thorns and thistles for you, and you will eat the plants of the field. By the sweat of your brow you will eat your food until you return to the ground, since from it you were taken; for dust you are and to dust you will return."

Genesis 3:17-19

"There are people in the world so hungry that God cannot appear to them except in the form of bread."

– Gandhi

Yesterday, we looked at the poverty we all experience. But not all poverty is the same.

The 300+ Bible verses that talk about poverty generally address economic poverty. We all experience broken relationships, but we don't all experience material poverty. We don't experience the devastation that arises from not being able to meet basic human needs or to realize one's God-given potential. "Low-income people daily face a struggle to survive that creates feelings of helplessness, anxiety, suffocation and desperation that are simply unparalleled in the rest of humanity," say the authors of *When Helping Hurts*.

Some people are more vulnerable than others to the risks of economic poverty. The Bible often talks of the widow, the alien, the victim, and the fatherless. What do these people all have in common? They are people on the margins of society, people who fall through the cracks, often because they don't have a solid support system—whether from their family, community or the wider society. Today, the list of those who live in poverty often parallels those mentioned in the Bible: refugees, minorities, single mothers, fatherless children and people with disabilities.

This is where our understanding of brokenness comes into play. Broken people in broken relationships create broken systems that lead to extreme poverty and systemic injustice.

It's hard for us to imagine, living in a society that highly values children, but the reality is that children are the most vulnerable group of all when it comes to poverty. When crisis strikes a nation—whether through famine, war or disease—everyone suffers, but children suffer the most.

Consider this: What if the entire population of the Greater Toronto Area was killed in one year due to diarrhea, respiratory infections, measles, and other causes that could have been easily remedied? It would be an unspeakable and unconscionable tragedy. That's roughly the number of children under the age of 5—5.9 million—who died in 2015, mostly due topreventable causes (World Health Organization).

Kemigisha is a mom in Uganda who is prone to malaria. She often gets severely ill with the disease, but does not have the resources to prevent it or treat it. That's why three of her babies have died while still in her womb. Her children in her womb were just as precious to her as they would be to a pregnant mother living in Canada. But these babies became just a few of the millions who die each year because of preventable causes.

Poverty isn't limited to the developing world either. In Canada, one in five children is growing up in poverty—and two in five aboriginal children live in poverty (Campaign 2000).

Melodie is a single mother raising a child in poverty. Less than two years ago, she had a full-time job, was in a relationship and had secure housing. But when she got pregnant, she made the difficult choice to leave her partner because of abuse. Her job as a welder was deemed unsafe for a pregnant woman, and she had to begin her maternity leave early, experiencing a gap in benefits. Now she's living in a trailer and struggles to provide for her baby through odd jobs and social assistance.

Globally, 10.7% of the world's population live in extreme poverty, defined as living on less than $1.90 per day (World Bank). Living on this little, it's impossible for parents to provide all that their children need. Many children aren't able to attend school or get health care. And more than 150 million children under the age of 14 work part time or full time (UNICEF). Think of that. That's more than the entire population of Russia—children who are forced to work in order to live.

Eleven-year-old Eliseo works from dawn to dusk to help his father harvest sugar cane in Mexico. The work is seasonal and his father earns very little, but his dad lacks the education to get a better job. So Eliseo has joined the ranks of the millions of children who work in order to help their families survive. "This is hard work; it is a hard life," says Eliseo's father. "Bearing the hot sun all day long is tough, especially for him, but there is no other way."

Poverty has many different faces. And behind every instance is a human longing for release from the struggle against their circumstances.

But the statistics are not all bad. Each year, the number of children who die before their fifth birthday drops thanks to interventions such as improved access to safe water, access to pre- and post-natal care and breastfeeding promotion. In fact, according to the UN, the number of children dying before age five plummeted by more than half between 1990 and 2015. The number of people living in extreme poverty is also dropping. Between 1990 and 2015, *one billion* people were lifted out of extreme poverty (UN). Gender equality is also moving forward with an equal number of girls and boys in secondary school (UN).

The reality of poverty is still bleak. But things can and are changing.

Reflection

Imagine what it would be like to live on less than two dollars a day—or even to eat on two dollars a day. How would you feel?

In what ways can broken relationships lead to economic poverty? What other factors might contribute?

When you read encouraging statistics—the enormous drop in extreme poverty rates and child mortality—what does it tell you about the problems of poverty?

Action

Extreme poverty is defined as living on less than $1.90 a day. Choose one day this week to eat using just $2 that day.

Prayer

I'm thankful, Lord, that You are all-knowing, all-loving, and all-powerful because sometimes it seems like our world is all-needing. I can easily be overwhelmed by numbers and statistics. Help me to remember that You care for each and every person and that You are already at work in this big, beautiful but broken world. Amen.

4 Finding Wholeness

"And Jesus grew in wisdom and stature, and in favor with God and man."
Luke 2:52

"Changed circumstances rarely change people's lives. Changed people inevitably change their circumstances."
— Compassion International

Poverty is complicated. Many of us would intellectually recognize this fact. But at the same time, we can have an overly simplistic view of people we encounter in poverty, thinking that if they just picked themselves up by their bootstraps, things could change.

Development expert Robert Chambers likens economic poverty to a spider's web with multiple interconnected strands: insufficient assets, vulnerability, powerlessness, isolation, and physical weakness. These factors can trap people until eventually they don't believe they have choices or can make changes. It's difficult to understand if you have never lived under the oppression of poverty, but living in this situation long enough, people can give up hope.

Michelle lived in the complex web of poverty. Born in a slum in the heart of Manila, Philippines, she lived in a small makeshift home shared by a total of seventeen relatives. Food was scarce and violence and drug abuse were common in the neighbourhood. Michelle's relatives eventually threw her drug-addicted father out, accusing him of theft. The anger of her relatives turned to Michelle because she looked like her father.

"You are so ugly," they taunted. "You will grow up to be like him."

A very young girl when she heard these words, Michelle came to feel that she was worthless and had no future. Like so many others, she began down the path of giving up. The messages that poverty had whispered in her ear—that she wasn't good enough, that she could never change her circumstances—began to take root.

When we recognize that those in poverty are real people with souls and struggles, like Michelle, we begin to realize that they want the same things we want. They want to be whole.

There's not much said in the Bible about Jesus' youth, but it does say in Luke 2:52, "Jesus grew in wisdom and stature, and in favor with God and man." Packed into this short verse is so much wisdom about what every person needs to thrive.

These are the factors that every person needs:
*   cognitive health (growing in wisdom),
*   physical health (growing in stature),
*   spiritual health (growing in favour with God)
*   and socio-emotional health (growing in favour with man).

Our response to poverty can't simply focus on the economic aspect, but rather it needs to take into account all these areas that make a person's life whole. A person needs educational opportunities and a conducive environment in which to learn, so that their minds can be healthy. A person needs their basic physical needs met so that they can grow to their full potential. A person needs to be spiritually healthy so that God's truth will take hold in their lives rather than the lies of poverty. And a person needs socio-emotional health, so they know how to form and maintain healthy relationships with others.

God wants wholeness and health for all of us.

The exciting thing is that wholeness can happen. In Michelle's life, it began when her aunt took her to church where she learned that Jesus loved her. Michelle says, "It was a simple but life-changing thought that would affect my whole destiny." The gospel began to change her identity from the daughter of a drug addict who could never change to the daughter of a God who had good plans for her life.

The changes continued when Michelle was sponsored by Christians from far away. They sent her letters that said, "You are very beautiful in our eyes. You are precious to us. We are praying for you." Michelle says, "These words touched the very depth of my heart and soul. God used them in healing my broken self-image and destroyed self-worth."

Michelle was able to pursue her dream of a degree in Communication Arts and then a Master's degree. She founded an organization that helps women who have been rescued from sex trafficking—affirming their worth and helping them grow into healthy, whole people. One key phrase she keeps in mind is, "You may have been born in poverty, but poverty was not born in you!"

Poverty is complicated and messy, but it doesn't have to be the final word. Michelle became a changed person, and she went on to change her circumstances and the lives of many. God is at work bringing people out of poverty and into lives that are healthier in every way.

Reflection

Think of yourself in Michelle's situation as a young girl. How do you think you would have reacted?

In Michelle's life, which of the four areas we discussed today were broken?

How do you think it would change your perspective on people in poverty if you stopped to consider their background story?

Action

Make a list of what wholeness looks like for you in terms of "wisdom, stature, favor with God and man." How similar is wholeness for you and for those living in poverty?

Prayer

Father, thank You that you see Michelle and you see me. You know our complex needs. You want wholeness and health for us. Help me to see as you do when I encounter people who live in economic poverty. Help me to see the ways in which they aren't so different than me, the ways in which we all depend on you. Amen.

The Hope of the World

"The Son is the image of the invisible God, the firstborn over all creation. For in him all things were created: things in heaven and on earth, visible and invisible, whether thrones or powers or rulers or authorities; all things have been created through him and for him. He is before all things, and in him all things hold together. And he is the head of the body, the church; he is the beginning and the firstborn from among the dead, so that in everything he might have the supremacy. For God was pleased to have all his fullness dwell in him, and through him to reconcile to himself all things, whether things on earth or things in heaven, by making peace through his blood, shed on the cross."

Colossians 1:15-20

"Poverty is rooted in broken relationships, so the solution to poverty is rooted in the power of Jesus' death and resurrection to put all things in right relationship again."

– Brian Fikkert

Looking at all the hard stuff going on in the world, it's easy to get tunnel vision—to start thinking everything is going to pieces. But as we read on day three, a lot of amazing progress is being made in ending extreme poverty. Much, though not all, of this progress is due to growing economies in places like China and India. While God is at work behind the scenes using economics and politics, we also recognize that He calls for a deeper solution to the complex roots of poverty. And we see that deeper solution in the person of Jesus.

Just as the actions of Adam and Eve brought sin, broken relationships, and death, so the actions of one man—Jesus—has resulted in life for all people. The death and resurrection of Jesus has the power to transform and heal these broken relationships that are at the heart of poverty.

When our relationship with God begins to mend, we learn to put the needs of others before our own needs. We begin to have His heart in fighting injustice and oppression. When God begins to heal people's relationship with themselves, people in poverty begin to reject the lie that they are worthless and should just give up, but rather begin to trust that God does have good plans for them. When God begins to chip away at the sin in our relationships with one another, we begin treating others as we would want to be treated and begin to bring healing to our communities. And as God begins to give us His eyes, we begin to see His creation not as something to be manipulated and exploited, but as something to be stewarded.

This transformation that God brings can look a lot of different ways.

It can look like Patience in Uganda who is fighting corruption in her local government. Patience's family was all killed by HIV/AIDS—her mother, her father and her three siblings. Patience was taken in by relatives who abused her and often didn't feed her. But Patience learned another way at her local church where she was registered in Compassion's program. She learned to stand for truth, integrity, and Christ. That's why when she graduated from university as a social worker, Patience decided to stand up to corruption. In her job in local government, she has been ensuring poor widows receive their annuities that had previously been denied to them by corrupt leaders. Because Jesus changed Patience's heart, she is now ensuring others don't fall into poverty.

It can also look like "Simon" in Canada. A former gang member, Simon lost a limb to an RCMP bullet, limiting his physical abilities and his ability to get a job. When he left penitentiary 10 years ago, he was addicted to heroin. But Simon connected with a church that puts the most vulnerable at its core. Church members began to walk alongside him, showing him that he can belong, and he is loved. Simon accepted Christ and was baptized. Although he's still rough around the edges, he's a changed man. Simon has been sober for seven years and oversees a moving company operated by his church.

It can also look like Ana, a young woman in Guatemala. After the trauma of multiple rapes at a young age, Ana felt unworthy, ugly, and unwanted. Because of the sin of another, her relationship with herself was broken. This led her to destructive behaviour, joining a gang so that she wouldn't ever be vulnerable again. "After I was raped, I got lost. I became a cold, violent criminal," she says.

It wasn't until she heard the healing words of the gospel that she realized she had worth: "I thought I was trash, but I am not. I learned that I have love in my heart." Ana began to believe that she was capable of changing her circumstances, and that God wanted good things for her life. Now, with the help of her church, Ana is taking steps to get out of poverty.

This is the mission of Jesus: to fix the mess we find ourselves in, and to set people on a good and healthy course. Jesus is the creator, sustainer and reconciler of all things. As it says in Colossians 1:19-20, "God was pleased to have all his fullness dwell in him, and through him to reconcile to himself all things, whether things on earth or things in heaven, by making peace through his blood, shed on the cross."

God is busy reconciling all things to himself. In stories like Patience's, Simon's, and Ana's, we see evidence that He truly is able to provide real, life-changing hope for all of us in all of our poverty.

Reflection

01
How does knowing that the ultimate solution to poverty is rooted in the death and resurrection of Jesus change your perspective on poverty?

02
Have you—or someone you know—experienced dramatic rescue by Christ from a lie that had entrapped you?

03
How do stories like those we read today extend your understanding of Jesus' work of reconciliation?

Action

Spend a few minutes thanking and praising God that He offers real, life-changing hope for people stuck in poverty through the death and resurrection of Jesus.

Prayer

Lord, the roots of poverty are complex. Broken relationships too often litter our lives. But You hold all things together. You are our Creator, our Sustainer and Reconciler. You are our hope. Thank You for all You have done and are doing in our world. Amen.

Seeing Ourselves

BIG PICTURE

This week, we'll come down from looking at the big picture and put the focus on our own lives because, to be honest, that's often where our blind spots lurk. Thinking about poverty through the lens of broken relationships and recognizing our own poverty changes everything. It isn't just about homelessness, hunger, or a lack of resources. It's about our own hearts and lives.

ADDITIONAL RESOURCES

- Groeschel, Craig. *Weird: Because Normal Isn't Working*. Zondervan, 2012.

- Platt, David. *Radical: Taking Back Your Faith from the American Dream*. Multnomah Books, 2010.

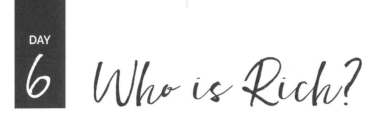

DAY 6

Who is Rich?

"Give me neither poverty nor riches, but give me only my daily bread. Otherwise, I may have too much and disown you and say, 'Who is the Lord?' Or I may become poor and steal, and so dishonor the name of my God."

Proverbs 30: 8b-9

"One of the most astounding things about the affluent minority is that we honestly think we have barely enough to survive in modest comfort."

– Ronald J. Sider

The definition of "rich" for many of us is "people who have more than we do." We probably all know someone who is richer than us—someone who can afford nice vacations, new cars, and a bigger house. When we hear of the inequality in the world between the wealthiest and the poorest, many average Canadians wouldn't think of themselves. As a consequence, we can easily skip past the verses in the Bible that address rich people, thinking they are meant for someone else.

Whether we recognize it or not, most Canadians are rich by world standards. In 2011, the average income after tax for an individual in Canada was $31,400. According to globalrichlist.com, this puts the average Canadian in the top 2 per cent of earners in the world. An annual net income of $42,000 puts you in the top 1 per cent.

There is a significant difference between the average lifestyle in Canada and living in extreme poverty, defined as living on less than $1.90 a day.

For example, think of what it takes to do your laundry. Most of us throw a load in the washer between other daily tasks or take a trip to a laundromat. In many parts of the world, however, doing laundry is a much bigger job. This task often falls solely to women. They may need to walk several kilometres to get to the nearest water source, toting large baskets on their way. Once they get to the river or pond, they soak their clothes regardless of the cleanliness of the water, scrub them by hand, wring them out, walk back home and hang the clothes to dry. The labour can take up to eight hours a week.

There's also a huge difference in how we cook our daily meals. In India, both urban and rural women spend time making cow-dung patties to use as cooking fuel. They collect firewood and drinking water, grind grains for food and preserve meat, as many don't have refrigeration. On average, they spend nearly six hours a day doing housework—work that we can complete in a fraction of the time with access to electricity, running water and labour-saving devices.

There are other measures of wealth: Do you own a bicycle or car? Is your roof made of dried leaves, corrugated metal, or something more sturdy that doesn't leak? Do you have a dirt floor or a finished floor? Do you have the means to eat meat or protein regularly? Do you have access to medical and dental care? Do you have running water and a waste collection service? In many contexts, all of these things we might consider basic necessities are considered luxuries.

The Bible doesn't condemn wealth in and of itself. Many people misquote 1 Timothy 6:10, believing it says that money is the root of all evil. In reality it says that "the love of money is the root of all evil." Being focused on wealth or "stuff" is what God condemns. He wants us to devote our wealth to Him just as He wants us to surrender every other part of our life to Him. That's what discipleship looks like. That's why when the rich young man approached Jesus eager to follow Him, but unwilling to give away all he had, Jesus said, "How hard it is for the rich to enter the Kingdom of God" (Mark 10:23).

While God doesn't command all of us to give away all our wealth to the poor, as Jesus directed the rich young man, Paul says, "Command those who are rich in this present world not to be arrogant nor to put their hope in wealth, which is so uncertain, but to put their hope in God, who richly provides us with everything for our enjoyment" (1 Timothy 6:17). God gives us good things "for our enjoyment"; it's not wrong to enjoy God's provision. But we put our hope in God, the Provider, and not in the provision itself. In the very next sentence, Paul writes, "Command them to do good, to be rich in good deeds and to be generous and willing to share" (1 Timothy 6:18). While God gives us good things for our enjoyment, at the same time, He commands us to do good, to be generous and willing to share. That's the balance each of us has to find as we seek Christ.

Wess Stafford, President Emeritus of Compassion International, offers wisdom when it comes to this balance: "The opposite of poverty isn't wealth. The opposite poverty is enough." The goal isn't to drag those with wealth into poverty, or for those living in poverty to become flush with riches. God wants us each to have enough. What does "enough" look like in your life?

God wants our hearts. He wants us to find our security and satisfaction in Him. He calls us to surrender all that we have—including our wealth—to His authority and purposes. And He calls each of us to live generously with our hands open to those in need.

Reflection

 Do you think of yourself as economically rich? How would thinking of yourself as rich change how you read the Bible and live your life?

 Is your security rooted in God or in wealth? How can you tell?

 What do you think "enough" might look like in your life?

Action

As you go through your daily routines, notice the "luxuries" you enjoy—and thank God for them.

Prayer

Lord, I am wealthy because my hope is secure in You. Thank You for the many ways You bless me and my family. I pray today for those who might work even harder than I do and yet struggle because of difficult life circumstances. Amen.

DAY 7 — The "Good" Life

"What good is it for someone to gain the whole world, and yet lose or forfeit their very self?"
Luke 9:25

"The real issue confronting us is whether the news of God's abundance can be trusted in the face of the story of scarcity."
– Walter Brueggeman

During the bombing raids of World War II, thousands of British children were orphaned. Some were rescued and placed in refugee camps where they received food and good care. But many of these children could not sleep at night. They feared waking up to find themselves once again homeless and hungry. Nothing seemed to reassure them. Finally, someone came upon the idea of giving each child a piece of bread at night. Holding their bread, these children could finally sleep in peace. Throughout the night the bread was a reminder that they would have food the next day.

We all need to feel a sense of security; it's a basic human need. The problem is where we find that security. In a culture dominated by individualism, materialism and consumerism, we clutch at our jobs, benefits, home, insurance, and retirement plan like the children with their bread. With every media message proclaiming that satisfaction is our right, we grab at our electronics, entertainment, cars, toys and travel, searching for the good life.

The problem is that when we are focused on the bread in our hands, we have very little time, money, or energy for anything else. We are concerned with our own security and needs, so we become desensitized to the needs of others. We avoid the article, change the channel, and ignore the tags on our clothes. Like the priest and the Levite in the story of the Good Samaritan, we pass by on the other side of the road (see Luke 10:32) rather than stopping to attend to the needs of others.

A few years ago, Candice and Daniel Chan of Calgary, AB, began wrestling with the dilemma of what the good life was really about when their small group started a study on the topic:

"On the surface, I was the ideal Christian," Daniel says. "But when we started the study, we faced a hard question: *who am I really living for?* I realized my dreams consisted mainly of ones that only had worth on this side of eternity: I pursued comfort and security, invested in hobbies and gadgets, acquired properties and traveled. We pursued savings and a retirement plan. We never would have said we were serving ourselves, but our actions revealed more than our words. It's subtle because our world tells us we can have it all. And when we're used to having more, we feel entitled to more."

Daniel became convinced that Christians are called to simple living and to simply live for Christ. "Sure there are exceptions, but the epidemic issue is that we all think *we* are the exception. Or we see that the Jones are doing this, and they are Christians, so I have the right to do this.

Simplifying their lives wasn't easy. Daniel recalled one day when he sensed God was asking him to sell his car: "A lot of my sense of achievement and pride rested in what I had, and I felt that people judged me on that basis. But God asked me, 'Is my love not enough for you? Are my promises not sufficient? My hope inadequate? My Son not enough?' Boy, that stung."

Generally, people either celebrated with the Chans as they made choices to simplify, or felt they had to justify the way they themselves were living.

"But that wasn't at all how I wanted to come across." Daniel insists. "I don't think there is a prescribed way we should live; it's not one size fits all. But I also think we don't think about this enough."

A practical approach for Daniel was to begin asking himself, "How would I spend money if it came from people within the church and from God?" He says, "So I still have a vehicle and a house, but the difference is that we try to spend or invest much like the way a missionary would to be accountable for what he or she's been entrusted. And if you think about it, we are all missionaries. When I'm making a purchase or a decision, I ask whether it will matter in five years, ten years or eternity. That makes it practical."

Living simply doesn't always mean austerity for Daniel either: "When it comes to building a relationship with my wife, for instance, I don't cheap out. It doesn't mean I'm extravagant, but building relationships matters in light of eternity."

Benedictine monks take a vow of poverty. They do so not because they believe material possessions are evil, but because they believe that living simply allows them to better listen to God. There is something to it. Have you ever felt that your stuff distracts you from God? That all the noise from your things—figurative and literal—keeps you from wholeheartedly focusing on God?

We are bombarded with messages that tell us we need to satisfy our wants— or even that our wants are, in fact, needs. But the message of Jesus is plain: "Whoever wants to be my disciple must deny themselves and take up their cross daily and follow me. For whoever wants to save their life will lose it, but whoever loses their life for me will save it. What good is it for someone to gain the whole world, and yet lose or forfeit their very self?" (Luke 9:23-25)

Jesus' words are scary. The lie that has been whispered in our ear is that there isn't enough; we aren't safe unless we are scrabbling to secure our own wants and needs. But Jesus asks us to let go of all that. Let go, and follow Him. Theologian Walter Brueggeman says, "The real issue confronting us is whether the news of God's abundance can be trusted in the face of the story of scarcity." Will we clutch our bread, or will we trust God to provide for us?

God knows our needs. He also knows our shortcomings and how we fall into fear. He offers us His grace and patiently leads us into the truly good life in Him.

Reflection

 Like the children in Britain who clutched their bread, what do you hold onto, worrying about tomorrow?

 Do you tell yourself a story of scarcity when it comes to your time and money?

 Do you think your material possessions have ever inhibited your ability to listen to God?

Action

Ask God if there are things in your life (material or otherwise) that you are clutching too tightly so that you aren't able to live generously or focus on Him. Consider giving away something of true value.

Prayer

Lord, in many ways I identify with the children who could only fall asleep when they held tightly to a piece of bread. Help me to examine what it is I clutch so tightly. I pray that You would work in me so that I might begin to trust Your story of abundance and provision. Amen.

DAY 8

The Upside Down & Backwards Life

"You know that those who are regarded as rulers of the Gentiles lord it over them, and their high officials exercise authority over them. Not so with you. Instead, whoever wants to become great among you must be your servant, and whoever wants to be first must be slave of all. For even the Son of Man did not come to be served, but to serve, and to give his life as a ransom for many."

Mark 10:42-45

"The way of the Christian leader is not the way of upward mobility in which our world has invested so much, but the way of downward mobility ending on the cross."

– Henri Nouwen

Jesus' early followers did not expect for a moment that He would die on a cross. They thought He was going to start a revolution and allow the Jews to triumph over their Roman occupiers. James and John even took Him aside to ask for special places next to Him in the new kingdom. Jesus explained that His kingdom was different: "Whoever wants to become great among you must be your servant, and whoever wants to be first must be slave of all. For even the Son of Man did not come to be served, but to serve, and to give his life as a ransom for many" (Mark 10:43-45).

Some people have described Jesus' kingdom as being backwards and upside down: the foolish things shame the wise and the weak confound the strong; the first will be last and the last will be first (1 Corinthians 1:27; Matthew 20:16).

Christ himself modeled this backwards and upside down life for us, "who, being in very nature God, did not consider equality with God something to be used to his own advantage; rather, he made himself nothing by taking the very nature of a servant, being made in human likeness. And being found in appearance as a man, he humbled himself by becoming obedient to death—even death on a cross!" (Philippians 2:5-8).

At the core, Jesus' life was about sacrifice and service rather than glory and honour, and that is what He calls us to. This means rethinking our idea of success and our belief that the opposite of economic poverty is wealth. It means rethinking that the North American way of life is the goal—for us or for those who live in poverty. Author and theologian Henri Nouwen called the way of Christ "downward mobility." If we are to be like Jesus, we too are to move downward—to serve and sacrifice.

This certainly turns the values of our society upside down. What might it look like to have an upside-down and backwards life in our society?

For Dominique Tremblay of Levis, QC, it looks like La Café Mosaique. Dominique and his wife began thinking about how faith could have an impact on day-to-day life in a neighbourhood. They decided to open a café as a way to serve their neighbours, a place that would be a "home away from home" where all would be welcome.

They asked themselves, "What are the values of the Kingdom of God?" This affected all their business decisions. Rather than purchasing less expensive products, they ensure the people who produce their food and drinks are fairly paid and treated with dignity. Rather than keeping profits for themselves, they decided to be non-profit, so they could invest in the good of the community. Rather than relying on the most socially acceptable people to run their café, they decided to put people from the margins at the centre of their business. Many of their volunteers are part of a restorative justice program, while others are referred by local psychologists as a way of making healthy connections in the community.

When Eugene Cho, author of *Overrated*, considered what God might want Him to do in order to serve others, God gave him a very clear direction: Give away the equivalent of a year's salary. Supporting a family on a pastor's salary, this was no easy request for Cho. But after continued prayer, he still felt called to give away one year's salary. It took several years and huge sacrifices for his family to meet this goal. Among some of the sacrifices, they sold his beloved car and even rented out their house while the family couch surfed. Some people thought he was crazy, but he was living the upside-down and backwards life.

God calls each of us to serve Him in a different way. For the Tremblays, following Christ meant making business decisions that were the opposite of what society would recommend. For Cho, it meant making considerable sacrifices to give away a large sum of money. For the Chans, whom we read about yesterday, it meant living a simpler life. These are all upside-down, Kingdom of God choices. It's not the kind of revolution Jesus' disciples expected, but as today's Bible passages show us, it reflects living a life in which others are first and we are last.

Living an upside-down life can be expressed in the smallest action as well as shaping our businesses, relationships and homes. When we shine the spotlight on our own lives, are they upside down and backwards, or do they look very much like the lives of everyone around us? We can begin today to invite God to invert our lives to be like Jesus' life.

Reflection

01 What do you fear in thinking about living in an upside-down Kingdom way?

02 What do you think the rewards would be of living in this way?

03 In what ways are you living upside down and backwards? In what ways could you?

Action

What is an action you can take today to practise downward mobility? Ask God to guide you to one action you can take today, such as serving someone who usually serves you.

Prayer

Lord, You certainly do things differently. If I really take Your Word seriously, I will live quite differently than the way our culture tells me to live. Help me to learn this upside-down way of seeing and living. Help me to become more like You. Amen.

DAY 9

The Fast God has Chosen

"Is not this the kind of fasting I have chosen: to loose the chains of injustice and untie the cords of the yoke, to set the oppressed free and break every yoke? Is it not to share your food with the hungry and to provide the poor wanderer with shelter—when you see the naked, to clothe them, and not to turn away from your own flesh and blood?"

Isaiah 58:6-7

"The Spirit wants to make you threatening to all the forces of injustice and apathy and complacency that keep our world from flourishing."

– John Ortberg

The people of God thought they had it all figured out. As Isaiah 58 records, they were religious people who held fasts and humbled themselves in sackcloth on spiritual days. They were performing their religious duties, so why didn't God seem to notice what good God-followers they were?

God made it very clear that He is not impressed with religious performances, but calls His people to deep, personal and genuine commitment on behalf of the poor and oppressed:

> "Is not this the kind of fasting I have chosen: to loose the chains of injustice
> and untie the cords of the yoke,
> to set the oppressed free
> and break every yoke?
> Is it not to share your food with the hungry
> and to provide the poor wanderer with shelter—
> when you see the naked, to clothe them,
> and not to turn away from your own flesh and blood?" (Isaiah 58:6-7)

The religious acts of the Israelites were empty and meaningless without a genuine concern for the well-being of others—for their families, the oppressed, the hungry, the wanderer and the naked. The religion God was interested in wasn't outward piety, but genuine compassion and a passion for justice. It was costly and took sacrifice.

Metro Community Church in Kelowna, BC, is learning what God's chosen fast might look like in their midst. Kelowna is a wealthy community that also happens to have the largest homeless population of a city its size in Canada. Few churches are in the centre of the city, where much of the need exists. Several Christians started hanging out downtown, and God began building a community. They wanted their Christian community to reflect the values of God, so they structured their church in what the world would consider an upside-down way.

"We believe the most vulnerable need to be held at our very centre, and we need to give them the loudest voice," says Pastor Laurence East. East noticed that in the Bible, God often speaks through the widow, the concubine, and the foreigner, so East and his church decided to listen.

Every significant decision about the community involves what East calls "the least likely" having a voice at the table, rather than being told they can't have power unless they conform.

This has sometimes been challenging for the middle-class Christians in the church who have had to learn to receive as well as to give, to love people rather than trying to fix them: "A lot of vulnerable folks don't believe from their own experience of church that God loves each person. They believe there are categories of worth based on what we do or don't do," says East. "It's equally a lesson for the most vulnerable and those who are middle class, and one learned best together, that we are made in His image and that is what makes us worthy."

Not only is this church responding to the needs of the vulnerable in their midst, as Isaiah 58 commands, but they are giving those who are usually on the fringes of the church a place of honour. They are giving a voice to those who have previously been voiceless, even when it it's challenging and takes away some of their own power.

The Church is called to respond to God's chosen fast, as Metro Community Church is, and we can respond in our individual lives as well. Allison Alley of Niagara, ON, was living the North American dream when God woke her up to His true fast.

"I was sitting at home, and I found myself inconsolable. Literally weeping," says Alley. "It was perplexing because at the time I had everything I had ever dreamed of: two beautiful and healthy children, a loving and supportive husband, a prosperous career in the finance industry and my dream home. And yet I came to realize that what was affecting me so deeply was that my heart was not aligned with God's. Painfully, I realized that I was more driven by consumerism, individualism, and success than serving or sacrifice. And so I began to realign my heart to His. Asking Him to break my heart for what breaks His."

Alley and her husband both felt God was calling them to care for children in need. They decided to sell their dream home and downsize their lives to live more generously—and also to symbolically walk away from their old way of life. Alley took a step of faith and left a successful career in finance to pursue a lifestyle of compassion and justice, which led to the opportunity to work for Compassion Canada. Today she uses her voice to raise awareness for the plight of children in poverty.

If you were to look at your own life, does your service to God include caring for the well-being of those in need and those who are suffering injustice? Do your religious acts cost you something, or are they superficial sacrifices like the fasting of the Israelites?

Few of us would say we're *for* injustice. No one wants to see people continue in slavery, prison, or oppression. But can we say that we are actively *for* justice? Do our actions reflect God's values or do they show us to be neutral? Is there even such a thing as being neutral?

This isn't about doing enough good to win God's favour. It's about God stirring our hearts. It's about God stirring up His people to rise up and fight for the most vulnerable around us.

Reflection

 **01** What verse in Isaiah 58 most stands out to you?

02 Stand back and look at your Christian life. How much of it involves outward Christian acts like the Israelites', and how much of it involves the chosen fast God describes?

03 How do you ensure that your acts to help others don't come from trying to win God's favour but are an expression of following Christ?

Action

Read all of Isaiah 58. Note the things God cares about and the promises He gives to His people who follow His chosen fast.

Prayer

Lord, I know that You aren't interested in outward piety. You care about my heart. You want my expression of faith to include caring for those who are vulnerable and oppressed. Thank You that You are patient with me, even when I get it wrong. Please give me Your heart for this world. Amen.

Renewal

"Therefore, I urge you, brothers and sisters, in view of God's mercy, to offer your bodies as a living sacrifice, holy and pleasing to God—this is your true and proper worship. Do not conform to the pattern of this world, but be transformed by the renewing of your mind. Then you will be able to test and approve what God's will is—his good, pleasing and perfect will."

Romans 12:1-2

"Our greatest fear should not be of failure but of succeeding at something that doesn't really matter."

– D.L. Moody

Sometimes we overcomplicate the life of faith. People have always done that—just think of the Pharisees who clung to their religious to-do lists to earn God's favour. Jesus, on the other hand, cut right through all the clutter and told us that two things really count: loving God and loving our neighbour.

We see God's love in the mercy offered to us through Jesus. And we flourish most when we respond to this love by centring our lives on God and extending love to those around us; when we place less security in things and more in Christ; when we surrender our whole lives for His purposes; when we're willing to abandon our comforts for Him.

If you've ever had a guitar or a piano, you know that over time it tends to get out of tune. You have to tune the strings to the right pitch—an A needs to sound like an A, and a D like a D. That's called recalibration. We all need to be recalibrated at times.

Sometimes, we are like the proverbial frog in the pot. If you place a frog in a pot of lukewarm water, he will stay in it. Turn the heat up slowly, and rather than jumping out, the frog will get used to the hot water until it's too late. Like the frog, we can also slowly get comfortable with the pot we're sitting in—the story the world tells us about ourselves and how we should live. We make one small choice to live like the world, then another, then another, until we realize that our lives are conformed more to this world than to the upside-down life Jesus modeled.

But God helps us see that, like a guitar or piano that's been played for years and gotten out of tune, we need to get back to the way He designed us to be. We need God's renewal.

In today's Bible passage, Paul reminds us of what God's renewal looks like: actively and intentionally resisting the patterns of the world and instead renewing our minds to engage in a new way of living. Here's how one man paraphrased Romans 12:1-2 in modern-day language:

"So here's what I want you to do, God helping you: Take your everyday, ordinary life—your sleeping, eating, going-to-work, and walking-around life—and place it before God as an offering. Embracing what God does for you is the best thing you can do for him. Don't become so well-adjusted to your culture that you fit into it without even thinking. Instead, fix your attention on God. You'll be changed from the inside out. Readily recognize what he wants from you, and quickly respond to it. Unlike the culture around you, always dragging you down to its level of immaturity, God brings the best out of you, develops well-formed maturity in you" (Eugene Peterson, *The Message*).

Have we become so well-adjusted to our culture that we fit in without even thinking? Does this describe what your own life looks like? Instead, God invites us to stop and fix ourselves on Him. We don't have to figure this out on our own. God will change us from the inside out, and He will show us what His will is for our lives.

Following Jesus means that we trade our vision for our lives for His vision; we ask to have eyes to see God's way for our lives. It means hearing what Jesus says when He tells His followers, "Do not store up for yourselves treasures on earth, where moths and vermin destroy, and where thieves break in and steal. But store up for yourselves treasures in heaven, where moths and vermin do not destroy, and where thieves do not break in and steal. For where your treasure is, there your heart will be also" (Matthew 6:19-21).

Our Western concept of happiness is focused on gratifying the self—storing up treasures here on earth. But we only flourish when we centre our lives on God. He is the source of everything that is good, pleasing, and perfect.

The world's mindset is one of scarcity, so therefore we accumulate all we can. But God's story is one of abundance—so how, therefore, should we live? If it's true that all we need can be found in Christ, how would we live differently from this world? As Christ followers, we can have peace. We don't have to chase what the world chases, but we can be at rest in Christ. As Christ followers, we can have joy in every circumstance. We know true joy is found only in God. As Christ followers, we can be generous; we know all our resources are God's to begin with. As Christ followers, we can be compassionate; we know that each person was crafted in God's image. As Christ followers, we can look to the needs of others rather than our own because that is what our Lord modeled for us.

As you reflect back on this week, what do you think God might be whispering, or even shouting, in your ear? Where have you stumbled and traded the world's vision for God's vision? Where have you been like the frog in the pot, slowly conforming to the pattern of this world? What might God be calling you to in your ordinary everyday life?

Place your "sleeping, eating, going-to-work, and walking-around life" in God's hands. Ask God to renew your mind and transform you from the inside out. Once again place your life and all that you have into His able hands.

Reflection

01 Looking at your daily life, do you believe your life is centred on God?

02 In what specific ways does your everyday life show love to people around you?

03 What step do you think God might want you to take in placing your trust and security in Him?

Action

Spend time in prayer about what God wants you to take away from this week's reading.

Prayer

Thank You, Lord, that it's You who is able to transform my mind. I admit that sometimes I slowly drift into becoming like this world. God, I give you myself, I give you my wealth, and I give you my heart. Please transform me to be like Jesus and show me what steps you want me to take. Amen.

Seeing God

BIG PICTURE

There is so much need around the world and in our own country, and so many competing ideas of how to respond. But God hasn't left us adrift without a guide. This week, we'll explore how the Bible reveals God's heart for the poor, and His plan to restore hearts and lives through the actions of His people.

ADDITIONAL RESOURCES

- David, Tom. *Red Letters: Living a Faith That Bleeds.* David C. Cook Publishing, 2007.

- Sider, Ronald. *Rich Christians in an Age of Hunger: Moving from Affluence to Generosity.* Thomas Nelson, 2005.

The Character of God

"He has shown you, O mortal, what is good. And what does the LORD require of you? To act justly and to love mercy and to walk humbly with your God."

Micah 6:8

"Overcoming poverty is not a gesture of charity. It is the protection of a fundamental human right, the right to dignity and a decent life."

– Nelson Mandela

Looking at all the hard things going on in the world, it's easy to ask, "Where is God? How can a good God allow so much suffering?"

If we look to the Bible, it assures us that God *is* good. Psalm 145:9 says, "The Lord is good to all; he has compassion on all he has made." From the very beginning, we see that God takes care of and loves His creation. He placed Adam and Eve in a garden where there was good food for them and good work to be done. After the Fall, God still provided for people, ensuring there was enough food and water that everyone could meet their basic needs.

The same is true today. God still provides, even in a world with more than seven billion people. He still makes "grass grow for the cattle and plants for people to cultivate" (Psalm 104:14). God cares for His creation. He cares for His image bearers.

But if God is such a good provider, if He really is so generous, what explanation do we have for the problems in this world? Why are so many living in poverty?

Has God failed? Has He forgotten the people He created?

The answer is a resounding no. Because we live in a fallen world, everything has been disrupted from God's original plan. But even though the world is not as it should be, we aren't to be resigned to this fact because God Himself is not resigned to it.

In Psalm 146:7-9, God is described in the following ways:
> He upholds the cause of the oppressed
> and gives food to the hungry.
> The LORD sets prisoners free,
> the LORD gives sight to the blind,
> the LORD lifts up those who are bowed down,
> the LORD loves the righteous.
> The LORD watches over the foreigner
> and sustains the fatherless and the widow,
> but he frustrates the ways of the wicked.

This is the character of God: He loves justice and pours out mercy. He loves the humble and protects the oppressed. He sees the widow and the orphan, the oppressed and those in need. He is the defender of the fatherless. He watches over the foreigner. He knows every need of those who are in distress.

And to meet those needs, He uses His people.

It's actually quite startling how often God talks about the poor, the hungry, the alien, the orphan and the widow—with more than 300 Bible verses on "the poor" alone. God made it very clear that He wants His people to reflect His goodness in this world.

In the Old Testament, we see commands to ensure those most vulnerable were protected. God commanded the Israelites to leave grapes and grain in their fields so that the poor and foreigners could glean from them (Leviticus 19:10; 23:22). He commanded the Israelites not to be "hardhearted or tight-fisted" toward the poor among them (Deuteronomy 15:7). He told them to seek their good and not take advantage of them (Exodus 22:21-22).

God reminded the Israelites to be open-handed with others because He was first open-handed toward them. He had brought them out of Egypt, a land in which they were mistreated and oppressed. Though they had done nothing to deserve it, God had blessed them, brought them to a good land and called them His own.

But God's greatest act of generosity came through Jesus coming into the world. God saw our greatest need and He held nothing back, giving His Son to rescue us: "For you know the grace of our Lord Jesus Christ, that though he was rich, yet for your sake he became poor, so that you through his poverty might become rich" (2 Corinthians 8:9).

God's generosity is the foundation of our own. Though we may not have vineyards and fields, we have still been abundantly blessed by God. Though, materially, we might have much or little, when we trust in Jesus, we are rich beyond measure. And what God calls us to do is to live generously out of His generosity—to see and act in light of His goodness and character.

This is what happened in the earliest days of the Church, as the first Christians came together. They saw one another's needs, and they did all they could to make sure there was no need among them. They held nothing back from one another (Acts 2:44-45). And that love, compassion, and generosity overflowed from among their own number and into the rest of the world.

Imagine what it might mean for us to live in this same way. Imagine how living as one who loves what God loves—mercy and justice—might change the choices we make each day. We could see our lives change in some extraordinary ways. After all, the opportunities to show compassion to those who are in need are all around us. We only need eyes to see.

Reflection

01 Read through today's Bible passages again and consider what they reveal to you about God's character and heart.

02 What are some modern equivalents to allowing the poor to glean the last grapes from a vineyard or the extra grain from a field?

03 Do you think your generosity comes from an overflow of God's mercy in your life? Why or why not?

Action

Grab a newspaper and a highlighter and read through the paper (or your online version), noting God's priorities as reflected in Micah 6:8 and Psalm 146:7-9. This might include a story about refugees or First Nations people or even a local story about justice.

Prayer

Father, Your Word tells us you are a father to the fatherless and a defender to widows. You are clearly a friend to the poor and oppressed. You see and grieve for people in slavery of all sorts around the world, and You invite us to be like You in both our hearts for the poor and our actions. Help us to see Your priorities clearly. Give us Your vision. Amen.

The Example of Jesus

"The Spirit of the Lord is on me, because he has anointed me to proclaim good news to the poor. He has sent me to proclaim freedom for the prisoners and recovery of sight for the blind, to set the oppressed free, to proclaim the year of the Lord's favor."

Luke 4:18-19

"Jesus showed his solidarity with the poor through his teaching, parables and lifestyle. It is no coincidence that in his very first recorded message he referenced the poor... Imagine God incarnate making his human debut and selecting one message from the Hebrew scriptures to begin his teaching... "The Spirit of the Lord is on me, because he has anointed me to preach good news to the poor."

– Mark Lutz

Think of the story of the woman at the well. Do you know it? Jesus is hungry and thirsty, and it's the middle of the day. It's hot. His disciples have gone looking for food. Jesus goes up to the well. Through the shimmering heat, he sees a woman there drawing water, and He decides to engage her in conversation. But here's the thing: most people didn't draw water in the heat of the day. This woman was at the well when no one else would be because she was ostracized by her own people. Maybe because she had had five husbands and now was living with another man. And the woman was a Samaritan, while Jesus was male and Jewish. That He even spoke to a despised person like her was exceptional.

And it was to this woman that Jesus spoke, explaining that He offered living water. It was in fact this woman—this nobody in her own society—to whom Jesus first revealed that He was the Messiah.

In our passage today, Luke 4, Jesus told the people of Nazareth he had come to proclaim good news to the poor and freedom to the oppressed. He always seemed to be noticing those that the rest of society pretended to be invisible— the woman at the well, a hated tax collector named Zaccheus sitting in a tree and, even as He was dying on a cross, he saw the need of the criminal who was being crucified next to Him.

Jesus offered them His living water, and He also offered them dignity, showing us that He came not just for the religious, but for those ignored and invisible to society. It didn't go over well with the religious leaders of the day. They said of Him, "Here is a glutton and a drunkard, a friend of tax collectors and sinners." (Luke 7:34) But Jesus provided a glimpse of God's heart for the world.

Jesus continually showed that He came to offer people His living water; He came for our souls and our spiritual well-being. But He also showed that He cared about the physical well-being of people. He cured diseases, he gave the blind sight, he fed the huge crowds who came to hear Him speak. John the Baptist wanted to know if Jesus was God's promised one, so he sent his disciples to ask. Jesus said to them, "Go back and report to John what you have seen and heard: The blind receive sight, the lame walk, those who have leprosy are cleansed, the deaf hear, the dead are raised, and the good news is proclaimed to the poor" (Luke 7:22).

Jesus could have simply said, "It is as you say," but He didn't. Instead, He pointed to His actions, as if to say, "Isn't it obvious; I am healing those in desperate need. This is what it looks like when the Son of God comes." Jesus' love expressed itself in both words of truth and actions of care and healing.

A life following and becoming like Jesus is one that offers wholehearted love for those in need. Kelly Cameron of International Justice Mission Canada recalls the start of her justice journey, a high school assignment where she had to create a project based on a current global issue: "It happened that the local paper was running a series of articles on 'child sex tourism' in Southeast Asia. This was before human trafficking was a known term and the UN's Palermo Protocol had not yet been drafted. My 16-year-old self was incensed at the fact that girls my age and even younger were being abused daily. And so began my justice journey. I don't consider it a coincidence that in the same year I started to pursue justice I also started to pursue Jesus."

Cameron went on to walk alongside teenage girls with addictions in California; women in crisis pregnancies in Ontario; sexually exploited children in Cambodia; and trafficked women and girls in Toronto. Cameron's life of following Jesus naturally overflowed into a life of advocating for those in desperate need.

Karen Stiller of New Song Church in Port Perry, ON, saw the photograph of the Syrian toddler whose body washed up on the shores of Turkey in September 2015. She heard about churches and community organizations sponsoring refugees, so Stiller turned to her husband and said, "Why can't we do that?" They invited others to get involved, eventually forming a group of five churches and community members who have raised more than $100,000 in a community of 9,500 people. They are in the process of bringing several refugee families to their community.

Stiller says they found a model for their actions in the life of Jesus, "He worked across boundaries, went outside of religious groups of his time, intentionally engaging with people who didn't fit in. This is the Church being the Church on a few levels—in response to God's call to care for the weak, vulnerable, orphans, and foreigners in strange land, and in that we are setting aside differences between churches, showing the world that we know Him through our love."

A life of becoming more like Jesus is a life given to serve others. It is a life caring for those we would have previously shrunk back from or simply ignored. Jesus calls us to follow His example and participate in bringing good news to the poor in our words and in our actions.

Reflection

 When we think of the Good News of Jesus, we often think of salvation. How do today's Bible passages potentially expand your definition of good news?

 What do you find most attractive and compelling about the way Jesus interacted with people?

 If Jesus came to your town, whom do you think He would be hanging out with?

Action

Who might be the woman at the well in your community? Take a step to show Christ's love to her.

Prayer

Lord Jesus, Thank You for coming into our world and moving in among us. Thank You for showing us through Your life and teaching what the love of God looks like. Give us the eyes to see as You see, and the compassion to feel toward people as You feel. Thank You. Amen.

The Role of the Holy Spirit

"But the Advocate, or the Holy Spirit, whom the Father will send in my name, will teach you all things and will remind you of everything I have said to you."

John 14:26

"Any transformational development that is not guided, empowered and made effective by the Holy Spirit will not prove sustainable. Furthermore, expecting and praying for supernatural interventions by the Spirit must be part of the spirituality of Christian development workers."

– Bryant Myers

Up to this point in your reading, you've taken a lot in. You've thought about the great needs in the world. You've thought of the commands of God to pour yourself out to the poor. You've reflected on Jesus' supernatural example of compassion and love. And you might just be feeling a little burdened by it all. There are so many needs, and God's bar for love is so high.

But one thing that we sometimes forget is that we have not been left alone to do it by ourselves. God knows we aren't able without Him. That's why when Jesus told His disciples He would be leaving, He promised them He would send someone to take His place: the Holy Spirit.

In John 14:15-17, Jesus says, "If you love me, keep my commands. And I will ask the Father, and he will give you another advocate to help you and be with you forever—the Spirit of truth." Jesus asks us to obey His commands, but at the same time He tells us that we have a Helper, a Spirit of truth who will guide us.

In John 14:26, Jesus describes what the Holy Spirit will do. The Amplified Bible puts this way: "But the Helper (Comforter, Advocate, Intercessor—Counselor, Strengthener, Standby), the Holy Spirit, whom the Father will send in My name [in

My place, to represent Me and act on My behalf], He will teach you all things. And He will help you remember everything that I have told you."

In all aspects of our Christian life, including serving those in need, the Holy Spirit is with us. He strengthens us when we feel weak or incapable. He teaches us and reminds us of the truth. He acts in our lives on behalf of Jesus to guide us. And He doesn't do this only for "us" living in relative wealth in Canada. The Holy Spirit is active throughout the world. He is the one moving in people's lives to transform them into Christ's image.

The evidence—or fruit—of the Holy Spirit's working in our lives are character qualities that reflect the character of the Father and the Son: love, joy, peace, patience, kindness, goodness, faithfulness, gentleness and self-control (Galatians 5:22-23).

It's the Holy Spirit who helps us see the homeless man sitting in the rain or to pray about a story we hear on the news. The same Holy Spirit also prompts us to act and gives us what we need to do God's will.

For Andrea Primmer of Toronto, ON, the Holy Spirit nudged or prompted her in a number of ways. On her first maternity leave four years ago, she sensed that nudging: "God was trying to get my attention about how tightly I was holding onto my identity as a professional." Primmer, who was trained as a physiotherapist, says, "It's a wonderful profession, and I'm proud of it, but my alignment and priorities were off. The picture that kept coming to my mind was that of a closed fist." After several months of wrestling with this, Primmer says she surrendered control of her identity to God, allowing Him to step in and do whatever He wanted.

Some time later, Primmer says, "I'd had a bit of practice with opening my hands around my profession when I began to sense that God wanted me to apply for a learning trip to [Lesotho] to visit programs our church has contributed to." For Primmer, this kind of trip had never been on her radar. It was expensive, there were potential health risks—and it meant leaving her two-year-old behind. She thought the biggest barrier would be getting her husband's support, so she asked God to open doors if this was His will. Her husband decided not only to support Andrea's decision but to join her on the trip.

Their trip to Lesotho had a tremendous impact on Primmer and her husband. They decided they wanted to continue to donate to global projects and also to get involved in their community as a family. Primmer began a moms' group for mothers who were struggling with isolation in her neighbourhood, and as a family, they began preparing, serving, and sharing meals a couple times a month at a home for refugees in the community.

"The Holy Spirit is mysterious and works differently in different people's lives," says Primmer. She sees the ways she and her husband have simplified their lives, largely by her letting go of her grip on her career as a way of creating space to hear God's quiet prompting: "God is always trying to get my attention, but I am only able to hear Him when I stop what I'm doing, when I stop worrying or stressing or fixating on whatever in my life is upsetting, and I create space for Him."

Following the Holy Spirit's leading to let go of her career wasn't easy for Primmer. But this first step of listening to the Holy Spirit and obeying began a domino effect of following God and serving others.

It can be easy to try to jump in and help people on our own, but Jesus reminds us that we can't: "I am the vine; you are the branches. If you remain in me and I in you, you will bear much fruit; apart from me you can do nothing." (John 15:5) We need to depend on the Holy Spirit to guide our actions, to strengthen us and to give us peace. We can also find relief in knowing that it is the Holy Spirit who is at work in other people's lives as well. We can't fix anyone, and our only job is to be faithful to what God's Spirit leads us to do.

Reflection

01 What do today's passages teach (or remind) you about the activity of the Holy Spirit in our lives and world?

02 How can you ensure that you are listening and sensitive to the Holy Spirit in your life?

03 How do you reconcile the role of people and God when it comes to work with people living in poverty? Do you tend to fall more on one side or the other—either believing that God will fix things or that it's up to us to fix things?

Action

Ask God to fill you with His Holy Spirit and make you sensitive to the nudging, comfort, and peace He gives.

Prayer

Heavenly Father, Jesus called Your Holy Spirit the "Helper." Help me make space for Your Spirit in my life, knowing that without Your Spirit, our work is hollow, ineffective and unsustainable. May I rely on You today. Amen.

DAY 14
The Role of the Church

"And let us consider how we may spur one another on toward love and good deeds, not giving up meeting together, as some are in the habit of doing, but encouraging one another—and all the more as you see the Day approaching."
Hebrews 10:24-25

"The church is the church only when it exists for others—the church can only call itself the church if its focus is outward and not inward."
– Dietrich Bonhoeffer

In a convocation address to the University of Toronto's Knox College, veteran CBC foreign correspondent, Brian Stewart, told of his experience with the Church:

> I've found there is no movement, or force, closer to the raw truth of war, famines, crises and the vast human predicament, than organized Christianity in action. And there is no alliance more determined and dogged in action than church workers, ordained and lay members, when mobilized for a common good. It is these Christians who are right "on the front lines" of committed humanity today and when I want to find that front, I follow their trail. It is a vast front, stretching from the most impoverished reaches of the developing world to the hectic struggle to preserve caring values in our own towns and cities. I have never been able to reach these front lines without finding Christian volunteers already in the thick of it, mobilizing congregations that care, and being a faithful witness to truth, the primary light in the darkness, and so often the only light.

From its beginning, the Church has been at the forefront of movements to respond to the needs of the most vulnerable people in the poorest communities around the world. The Early Church declared that wherever a church building was built, a hospital would be built as well to care for the needs of all people. It was the Church that took responsibility for education, keeping alive language, literature, and culture in the Dark Ages. It was the Church that developed schools for impoverished British children in the nineteenth century. And it was voices from within the Church who fought for the abolition of slavery in the British Empire.

In His time on earth, Jesus founded one organization: the Church. He didn't found or commission any other agency to advance His Kingdom on the earth. And this Church is unstoppable. Jesus said in Matthew 16:18, "the gates of Hades will not overcome it." This organization, left to and still populated by a "ragtag bunch," has continued for nearly two thousand years, stretching to every corner of the globe. This Church has been dynamically moving throughout history. It is the largest organization on earth with hundreds of millions of members and the ability to mobilize millions of volunteers and countless resources.

The Church is uniquely positioned to care for the needs in the world. Local churches are the ones who are close to their communities and understand the local culture. They are also known by their communities and can build trust in a way that outsiders cannot. They know what the real needs are and have a deeper understanding of what will work and will not work in their context. They are there for the long-term—long after any foreign aid will be there. They are the ones who can offer not only physical help, but also spiritual healing. They, as Hebrews 10:24 states, can "spur one another on toward love and good deeds."

George Lusana Zablon is a pastor in Tanzania whose church is a light in the darkness. Not only does the church preach the gospel to the community, but through their partnership with Compassion they also respond to the myriad physical needs in their community where most people live in extreme poverty. "In this way, the church is seen as acting in love," says Zablon. "Through the acts of love, the church becomes strong and it is respected in the community. In the middle of suffering and difficulties, the church should show love—not just mere words of love, but love in action. People can see that God is a God of love and He is a God of love with action."

Through being shown Christ's love not only in words but also through acts of compassion, countless people have surrendered their lives to Jesus. And it is not only people with plenty who can minister to those in need. It is a reciprocal relationship.

Pastor Brad Somers describes his congregation, PAXnorth Church in Halifax, as a "mixed bag in their faith journeys" with members who are homeless or who use food banks and soup kitchens, as well as young professionals, artists and academics, former prostitutes and addicts. It very much sounds like the rag-tag bunch who followed Jesus.

While PAXnorth benefits from members who have experienced stability, ministry doesn't just come from the professionals to the street people. Somers talks about a church member struggling with drug addiction, saying, "As much as he needs us, we need him." He observes that the churches in the book of Revelation that look like they have it all together are the ones God calls poor, weak and empty (Revelations 2, 3). He adds, "Someone like this can show our church deeper realities of what it means to depend only on Christ."

The local church is the hope of the world because it is through the Church that people will find our true source of hope: Jesus. Only the Church can address poverty at its root level. Only Jesus can bring true wholeness to a person's life. And the Church is God's chosen instrument to bring this healing and hope to the world.

Reflection

 When we are tempted to bail out on the church as an institution, what does the fact that Jesus had no back-up plan besides the church tell you?

 What has characterized your best experiences of being part of the church?

 What is the church able to do to bring hope to people in need that individuals are unable to do?

Action

Sometimes we forget the value of the church. Today send a quick note of appreciation to your pastor or someone else who has helped build the church's role in your life.

Prayer

Lord, when I think about the idea that you don't have a backup plan for your mission on earth, it encourages me to put down deeper roots in the Church You love. Help me to have Your vision for the Church both locally and globally and to recognize the role we have as believers together in offering hope to a broken world. Amen.

The Two Greats

"This is how we know what love is: Jesus Christ laid down his life for us. And we ought to lay down our lives for our brothers and sisters. If anyone has material possessions and sees a brother or sister in need but has no pity on them, how can the love of God be in that person? Dear children, let us not love with words or speech but with actions and in truth."

1 John 3:16-18

"Anyone wanting to proclaim the glory of Christ to the ends of the earth must consider not only how to declare the gospel verbally but also how to demonstrate the gospel visible in a world where so many are urgently hungry."

— David Platt

The idea that the Church should be on the frontlines of ministry to people in need is not new, but there has always been a tension between the good news and good works. We can see this tension even in the first century as James asks, "What good is it, my brothers and sisters, if someone claims to have faith but has no deeds? Can such a faith save them?" (James 2:14)

In North America, this tension was heightened in the nineteenth century with the rise of the Social Gospel movement. This movement promoted humanitarian efforts as bringing about God's Kingdom, and tied salvation to good works rather than the true change of heart that is at the core of salvation. But as so often happens when a group swings too far in one direction, as a response, another group swings too far in the opposite direction. In an effort to reject a false gospel of good works and to distance themselves from liberal theology, many Christians in North America swung away from ministry to those in most need, instead focusing on evangelism.

The focus of many churches shifted away from corporately supporting ministries of mercy. Instead, they emphasized evangelism and individual conversion and sanctification. They backed away from the activities the Church had always been involved in, such as ministries to provide things like food, education, and health care to the neediest in their communities.

But the Holy Spirit is always at work. The Church has been awakening to the truth that we don't have to choose between faith and deeds. Indeed, the Great Commission and the Great Commandment go hand-in-hand.

Jesus revealed His Great Commission to the Church in Matthew 28:19-20:

> "Therefore go and make disciples of all nations, baptizing them in the name of the Father and of the Son and of the Holy Spirit, and teaching them to obey everything I have commanded you. And surely I am with you always, to the very end of the age."

Our mandate to make and baptize disciples is clear. The second part of the commission is to "teach them to obey everything I commanded you." So what are the commandments Jesus taught?

In Matthew 22, Jesus revealed what the Greatest Commandment is. An expert in the Law, hoping to trip Him up, asked Jesus which was the most important commandment. Jesus answered, "'Love the Lord your God with all your heart and with all your soul and with all your mind.' This is the first and greatest commandment. And the second is like it: 'Love your neighbor as yourself.'" (Matthew 22:37-39)

Inherent in the Great Commission is loving God and loving our neighbours as ourselves. How do we love our neighbours? An expert in the Law wanted to know this too, so He asked Jesus "And who is my neighbor?" (Luke 10:29) Jesus' response is the famous parable of the Good Samaritan. In this story, Jesus tells of a Jewish man who is robbed, beaten, and left for dead. Although others chose to pass him by, a Samaritan—a people group hated by the Jews—chose to stop and care for the needs of the man. He took pity on him, bandaged him, put him on his donkey, took him to an inn, and paid for him to stay and be cared for there.

That's what it means to love your neighbour—to care for the needs of the people we encounter, even across religious and cultural lines. And that's what it means to follow God's commands, as the Great Commission directs us.

And, as we have already seen, because the root causes of poverty are spiritual and only Jesus can bring true healing to a person, it is the Church who can respond to the deepest needs of those living in poverty.

Reverend Everett Swanson was a pastor from Chicago, Illinois, who faced this very real tension between the good news and good works. He traveled to South Korea during the Korean War to preach the gospel to soldiers. But while he was there, he witnessed something he could not forget. He saw countless children orphaned by the war living—and dying—on the streets. He saw their bodies being tossed into trash trucks like yesterday's garbage. Having seen this, Swanson knew he had to act.

As he flew home, he heard a voice repeating in his mind to the rhythm of the airplane jets, "What are you going to do? What are you going to do? What are you going to do?" When Swanson got home, he rallied Christians to donate money to start an orphanage for these children whose parents were killed by war. This ministry grew until it eventually became Compassion International. Today, Compassion connects Christians with thousands of churches in the developing world who are bringing both opportunities to escape poverty and the light of the gospel to millions of children.

As we follow Christ and grow deeper in His love, that same love will overflow from us to others. As the Church, we have been called, redeemed and equipped to bring God glory through making disciples, loving Him and loving others as ourselves.

Reflection

 Between the good news and good works, to which side do you sometimes tend to lean?

 In what way are the good news and good works intertwined?

 If people living in poverty looked at your church, where might they see the love of Jesus being offered to their needs?

Action

Today when you see someone in need, be like the Good Samaritan and offer help, whether that is in the form of a conversation or an offer of physical support.

Prayer

Lord, as humans, it's easy for us to lean too far in one direction or the other. Would you please use Your Holy Spirit to guide us? Help us to embrace both Your Great Commission and obey your Greatest Commandments. Amen.

Seeing Others

BIG PICTURE

It's easy to find ourselves using "us" and "them" language when we think about people living in poverty, but we are all the same as human beings created in God's image. This week, we will be challenged to examine how we see others—and how we act toward them as a result.

ADDITIONAL RESOURCES

- Greenfield, Craig. *Subversive Jesus: An Adventure in Justice, Mercy, and Faithfulness in a Broken World.* Zondervan, 2016.

- Lutz, Mark. *UnPoverty: Rich Lessons from the Working Poor.* UnPoverty Communications, 2010.

Perceptions of the Poor

"Listen, my dear brothers and sisters: Has not God chosen those who are poor in the eyes of the world to be rich in faith and to inherit the kingdom he promised those who love him?"
James 2:5

"I had come to see that the great tragedy in the church is not that rich Christians do not care about the poor but that rich Christians do not know the poor... I truly believe that when the rich meet the poor, riches will have no meaning. And when the rich meet the poor, we will see poverty come to an end."

– Shane Claiborne

Have you ever met someone famous? Apparently, it's not uncommon for people to faint when they meet the Queen. Even passing someone well-known on the streets causes us to get excited.

In the book of James, God invites us to consider a couple of scenarios: "Suppose a man comes into your meeting wearing a gold ring and fine clothes." (James 2:2) How do we react? Do we, as James suggests, "show special attention to the man wearing fine clothes and say, 'Here's a good seat for you'" (v.3)? If we're honest, many of us might. If some famous or clearly wealthy person comes into our church, chances are good that we will treat that person with honour. But there's another scenario in James: "A poor man in shabby clothes also comes in." James suggests we often say to the poor man, "You stand there" or "Sit on the floor by my feet" (v.3).

When we do this, James says, "Have you not discriminated among yourselves and become judges with evil thoughts? Listen, my dear brothers and sisters: Has not God chosen those who are poor in the eyes of the world to be rich in faith and to inherit the kingdom he promised those who love him? But you have dishonored the poor" (James 2:4-6).

Do our attitudes toward the poor dishonour them? If so, it's no small matter. James says we have become "judges with evil thoughts." When you see someone who looks poor or homeless enter your church, what thoughts go through your mind? When you see someone at the store or on the street who looks poor, what assumptions come to mind?

The Salvation Army surveyed Canadians to understand our perceptions of people living in poverty. They found that "the vast majority of Canadians do believe that everyone, despite their socioeconomic status, deserves dignity and most agree that the poor deserve a helping hand. The bad news is that many believe that the poor have mostly themselves to blame and that poverty is a choice." Among the survey findings, this belief expressed itself in a variety of ways:

- Nearly half of all Canadians feel that if poor people really want to work, they can always find a job.

- About a quarter of Canadians feel that people are poor because they are lazy and have lower moral values than average.

- 96 percent of Canadians believe that everyone deserves a sense of dignity, but only 65 percent believe that being poor can rob you of dignity.

Do you believe that being poor can rob a person of dignity? If you were treated as if you were invisible or as less valuable than the rest of society, what impact do you think that would have on you long-term?

While sometimes people living in poverty in Canada are treated as less worthy than others, we can see people living in poverty in developing nations as objects of pity. We consider them helpless and pathetic rather than acknowledging their skills and potential. Because we view them as helpless, we treat them as projects, as if we can do with them as we see best.

Each human was made in the image of God. Each person was crafted to bring God glory in their unique gifts and abilities. And, as James says, "has not God chosen those who are poor in the eyes of the world to be rich in faith?" What if, instead of coming to the table with all of our preconceptions, we simply got to know people living in need? As Shane Claiborne says, "I had come to see that the great tragedy in the church is not that rich Christians do not care about the poor but that rich Christians do not know the poor."

Blythwood Baptist Church in Toronto has offered an Out of the Cold program for the past 21 years. Pastor Abby Davidson says, "It's not just about a meal and a place to sleep. We sit with people, have dinner with them, talk with them, find out their names and how we can pray or offer support."

Those living in poverty are people, not problems. They are our neighbours, not numbers. Before we can begin to help others, we need to recognize that people living in poverty are real people with real names, gifts, and abilities. They are people as worthy of dignity as we are. They are people whom God created with a purpose in mind.

Reflection

01 How many friends do you have who live in poverty? Why do you think this is?

02 In what ways do you think your perception of people living in poverty needs to change?

03 What specifically might you do to treat a person living in poverty with dignity and demonstrate the love of God to that person?

Action

Make a list of all the adjectives you have heard to describe people who are poor. Does this list describe people you know living in poverty?

Prayer

Lord, I confess to You that sometimes my perceptions of the poor are either stereotypical or ones where I look down on people living in need. Would You give me fresh eyes to see people around me as people with names, families, stories, resources and gifts? Amen.

DAY 17 *Identity*

"For you created my inmost being; you knit me together in my mother's womb. I praise you because I am fearfully and wonderfully made; your works are wonderful, I know that full well."
Psalm 139:13-14

"You cannot have a more powerful word to describe the cure for poverty or for empty hearts that should be reaching out to poverty than hope."
– Wess Stafford

We've considered what poverty really is—that it isn't merely a lack of money, but has to do with broken relationships. Have you ever wondered how people actually living in poverty might define it?

When a group of women in rural Rwanda who live on less than two dollars a day were asked how they defined poverty, their top answers were:

1. Poverty is an empty heart
2. Not knowing your abilities or strengths
3. Not being able to make progress
4. Isolation
5. No hope or belief in yourself

No one mentioned a lack of money, lack of access to clean water, lack of nutrition or education. And this definition of poverty is not limited to this small group. Several years ago, researchers from the World Bank asked the same question to more than 60,000 people living in poverty—people they called "the true poverty experts"—and the answers were strikingly similar.

Their answers also sounded a lot like the broken relationships we talked about a few weeks ago. They described poverty in terms of suffering relationships, a lack of belonging and a lack of dignity. To them, poverty was a feeling of hopelessness, voicelessness, worthlessness, and powerlessness.

"Jack" had been in and out of jail various times before he started a relationship with a young woman. When she became pregnant, it was a wake-up call: he got a job and faithfully went to work for the next few months. Then he got sick and missed a few days of work. Suddenly, he began to unravel. He stopped going to work and stopped making changes. He fell back into old, negative patterns. Though it might seem inexplicable to those of us who have never lived in poverty, for Jack, poverty was a lie that whispered, "There is no hope. You might as well give up," and he began to live accordingly.

The tragedy of poverty is not just that people don't have access to adequate food, clean water, education, housing, medical help or opportunities, but that, additionally, people are degraded and dehumanized, losing a sense of dignity, hope and identity. Mother Teresa says, "The poverty of being unwanted, unloved and uncared for is the greatest poverty."

What a contrast to what God says about each and every person in Psalm 139, that we are created in God's image—fearfully and wonderfully. Every person has dignity and worth, gifts and purpose.

How we understand poverty plays a major role in our attempts to alleviate that poverty: it can be like the difference between a doctor treating symptoms or the root cause of a disease. When it comes to poverty, we can add to the sense of shame and inferiority of the poor by simply throwing money at their needs. By contrast, we can value people who live in poverty by offering them hope and dignity, and also by recognizing their significant intelligence, skills, and resources.

Michael Turner is an artist who works in encaustic or colourful wax art. Born in Montreal, Michael grew up in a strict family before being taken away at the age of six and placed in a Catholic boys' home, where he was abused by a priest. These experiences haunted him for years, leaving him with pain, disappointment, and self-blame. For the last couple of years, Michael found himself homeless in Winnipeg. But he became connected with Siloam Mission, a Christian humanitarian organization that alleviates hardships and provides opportunities for change for those affected by homelessness. The organization has an art program, and Michael got involved.

Through creating art, Michael has found hope. The peace he has found in his art, along with his faith in God, have given him a dream, a strong sense of purpose and personal healing. He learned that he is worthwhile and he has something to offer. He has built community with staff, volunteers and those who admire his work. "I truly believe that this is what our Father had in mind for me," Michael says of his art. "This has given me a sense of peace that I have never experienced before." The Siloam community notes that in turn, Michael has "given our community the gifts of colour, encouragement, and hope."

Just because someone doesn't have money doesn't mean they have nothing to give. A church in Uganda built a well where the community could access safe water. Community members could buy water for a small fee that was pooled for the maintenance of the water source. The fee was only a few cents, but it was too expensive for some of the community members who were subsistence farmers. The church decided that instead of contributing financially, these community members could be responsible for cleaning the well and tap stand. These families took great pride in ensuring that it was clean and well maintained. One of the engineers who helped with the project said, "You've never seen such a clean well in your life." Though these families didn't have material resources to give, they still were valuable contributors.

Truly seeing people in poverty means both recognizing the deep and complex factors in their psyches that keep them stuck in poverty, as well as the deep and complex gifts and resources each one possesses as people created in the image of God.

Reflection

01 Now that you're more than halfway through this resource, how would you define poverty?

02 Do you believe that each and every person is "fearfully and wonderfully made" with worth and dignity? In what situations is it a challenge for you to believe this?

03 Re-read the list of how the Rwandan women described poverty. What sticks out to you most? How would your response to poverty change if this is how poverty really affects a person?

Action

Spend time in prayer, repenting of attitudes that keep you from seeing the poor as they are, and from wanting to apply quick material fixes to complex relational problems.

Prayer

Lord, I believe, but help my unbelief. I believe that each and every person is made in your image, but like people in economic poverty, I sometimes struggle to believe that I am worthwhile, let alone others. Sometimes it's hard to see that beautiful image in some people. Give me new eyes to see both the deep hopelessness some people living in poverty face and the beautiful image of God in them. Amen.

The North American Saviour Complex

"For Christ's love compels us, because we are convinced that one died for all, and therefore all died. And he died for all, that those who live should no longer live for themselves but for him who died for them and was raised again. So from now on we regard no one from a worldly point of view. Though we once regarded Christ in this way, we do so no longer."
2 Corinthians 5:14-16

"A self-sufficient human being is subhuman."
– Archbishop Desmond Tutu

There's an Instagram account by the name of "Barbie Savior." A satirical page, it posts pictures of a Barbie doll "saving" Africa and taking "slumfies" (that's "slum" + "selfie") while she's at it, posed heroically against the backdrop of need. Her tagline says, "It's not about me...but it kind of is."

Sometimes, us North Americans can see ourselves as the saviours of people in poverty. It's easy to fall into this way of thinking, especially in a time when fighting injustice is trendy. While this desire to save others is often accompanied by heartfelt compassion, we have to examine our motives. Do we want to help others so that we can feel good about ourselves? So that we can accomplish something great? So that we look good to others?

Is our service about serving God, or is it really all about us?

Judy Zacharias volunteers with a team from her church, Elevation, in Waterloo, ON, taking meals to Supportive Housing of Waterloo (SHOW), an organization that provides housing and support to those who have experienced homelessness. She reflects on her experience:

When I was a teen, I thought someday I would go out and "help people" in dire straits. They would be uplifted and encouraged by my being in their lives. I would do "big" things. Then I grew up and found out that is not how the world operates.

At SHOW, we eat with anyone who wants to join us. It is not pretty. It is not glamourous.

"Dan", who smells of cigarette smoke and a lack of showering, tries to converse intelligently, with big ideas trapped in a genius brain that has been damaged by alcohol abuse. Some nights we wonder about our safety as he yells at us. Other times, he can be very respectful and thankful.

"Rose" (who doesn't seem to like me much but loves my friend Helen), busies herself as the hostess she is, sometimes adding to the meal with things she has cooked. I find myself feeling a little envious of Rose and Helen's relationship.

"Lawrence" sometimes joins us if he can get beyond his nervousness, fear, and guilt. Others load up on food and disappear without a word.

This place is gritty, raw, and real. No two nights are the same. We never know what to expect. Sometimes I go home exhausted from listening to the same old stories, and wondering how better to connect with these people that I am supposed to be showing Christ's love to. Other nights I am encouraged at the small milestones in these broken lives.

I also see that their brokenness and my brokenness are not that much different.

When we go beyond our desire to be saviours, we begin to see those in poverty not as victims but as people. We begin to recognize our similarities and our equality as human beings loved by God, regardless of the differences in our bank accounts or life experiences. When we begin to see that poverty is often a result of unjust and broken systems, we begin to see our actions not as charity, but as acts of justice. We begin to see those in poverty not as charity cases, but as fellow humans deserving justice.

Doing so allows us to have two-way relationships. The relationship between hero and victim is one-way—only the hero has something to give. The assumption is that the hero doesn't need anything from anyone else. But as Archbishop Desmond Tutu so succinctly put it, "a self-sufficient human being is subhuman." All of us are in need of some sort or another and all of us have something to give. When we are willing to step out from this façade of hero with it all figured out, we realize that both parties have much to give and much to gain from one another.

When the wildfire in Fort McMurray, AB, raged in 2016, Syrian refugees, who had only been settled in Canada months before, knew how those who had lost everything in the fire felt. "It's not easy to lose everything," says Rita Khanchet, a Syrian refugee who now lives in Calgary. "We can understand them more than anyone in Canada," reported the *Calgary Herald*. Although they had so little, a group of Syrian refugees decided to pool their resources to help victims of the fire. The group decided to each give $5 towards purchasing hygiene items for evacuees. They are proof that everyone has something to give—even war refugees living in a foreign land.

Recognizing that we aren't saviours but that our hope is in our Saviour, Jesus, eliminates the artificial "us and them" thinking. That's what the passage from 2 Corinthians above teaches us: that Jesus died for all of us. This humbles us and invites us to enter into relationships with all people as our peers. We all need God's mercy and grace. Changing the way we think about ourselves also allows us to relax in our own imperfections and needs: we don't have to wait until we have it all together before we reach out to people in poverty—because we will never have it all together.

At the same time, the passage from 2 Corinthians reminds us Christ's death on our behalf means that we "no longer live for [our]selves but for him" and that as a consequence, "we regard no one from a worldly point of view." We can and are called to reach out to others, not as heroes, but as human beings on the journey together.

Reflection

01 In what ways does a desire to help people in poverty come out of a place of your own need?

02 Do your motives have to be entirely pure before you can serve or is that part of believing you really are a hero?

03 How does it feel to consider being a peer to people in poverty?

Action

Make a list of the reasons why you want to help people living in poverty—and be brutally honest with yourself. Then pray through the list with God.

Prayer

Father, it's awkward and humbling to admit that sometimes I unconsciously see myself as a hero. Would you help me instead to see You as the hero, and me as equal to all the people around me, equally in need of Your grace and hope? Amen.

Community

"They devoted themselves to the apostles' teaching and to fellowship, to the breaking of bread and to prayer. Everyone was filled with awe at the many wonders and signs performed by the apostles. All the believers were together and had everything in common. They sold property and possessions to give to anyone who had need. Every day they continued to meet together in the temple courts. They broke bread in their homes and ate together with glad and sincere hearts, praising God and enjoying the favor of all the people. And the Lord added to their number daily those who were being saved."

Acts 2:42-47

"Community is not an ideal; it is people. It is you and I. In community we are called to love people just as they are with their wounds and their gifts, not as we would want them to be...It means also receiving from them so that we too can grow."

– Jean Vanier

"There's no I in team" they tell us, but they also say "if you want to do something right, do it yourself." Anyone who has ever done a group project at school, been on a sports team or a committee understands this tension between individual and community. And there is no one right answer: we live life both as an individual and as a member of a larger group.

That said, different cultures lean different ways when it comes to this tension. Canadian culture is inclined toward an individualistic mindset. Each person's goals and achievements are considered important, and we value competition. We believe each person has an opinion that matters, regardless of who they are.

Compared to more communal focused cultures, we identify more with our friends and family than with society at large.

On the other hand, it is often our individualistic culture that disconnects us from one another and leaves us with what researchers describe as an epidemic of loneliness. A 2012 Stats Can report found that about 20 percent of older Canadians describe themselves as lonely, while in a study of 34,000 Canadian university students, two-thirds reported feeling "very lonely" in the past twelve months.

While individualistic cultures include places such as Canada, the UK, Australia, and the United States, the majority of the world's cultures are collective, including much of Africa, Asia, Central America and South America. Collective cultures emphasize the group over the individual, so people value selflessness and sacrifice for the common good. Loyalty and helping one another are key values, and collective cultures recognize the interconnectedness of all people. On the other hand, collectivist culture can result in conformity, group-think and what we might see as over-involvement in people's private lives.

The contrast between the two mindsets was clearly seen by a missionary flying home from Haiti. The plane was half-empty so the pilot invited anyone who wanted to change seats to do so. The missionary observed that every single North American got up and moved away from the people they were sitting with in order to have more personal space, while all the Haitians got up and moved closer to one another, whether they knew each other or not.

Finding a godly balance between individualism and being community oriented means exploring the less familiar side of the tension, which for many of us in Canada is community.

God created human beings to be in relationship, not in isolation. The only thing in the Garden of Eden that God said was not good was that Adam was alone. Galatians 6:2 reminds us to "carry each other's burdens and in this way you will fulfill the law of Christ."

Pastor George Lusana Zablon from Tanzania, whom we read about on day 14, is an amazing example of living in community. Although he only has two children, he often has up to 11 people living with him. Children whose parents have died or children who have been rejected for becoming Christians have come to live with him. When someone in the community has a need, they know his door will be open. Caring for all these needs often overwhelms him. But when Pastor Zablon begins feeling this way, he thinks to himself, "What would Jesus do in this situation? Would he deny them? No, he would welcome them to Him."

What would happen if, like Pastor Zablon, we extended our view of family and community? In 1964, Canadian Jean Vanier decided to do just that. Concerned about the institutionalization and isolation of people with intellectual disabilities, he invited two men from an institution to live with him in a small house he called "L'Arche," or "the ark" after the story of Noah. Today there are 29 L'Arche communities across Canada where people with intellectual disabilities live together with non-disabled individuals who share life in family-like settings. Living at L'Arche gives people the opportunity to reach their full potential in a place where they are seen as contributors and valuable members of the community.

L'Arche follows the model provided by the Early Church described in Acts 2:42-47. They fellowship together, eat together and share what they have when anyone has need. The Early Church knew the importance of living interconnected with one another, relying on the unique gifts each had to contribute. The truth is that today we are still part of the global family of Christ; we cannot be concerned only with ourselves. And the majority of our extended family lives in great need.

We need to allow others into our neat and tidy world. To recognize that God has called us to carry one another's burdens. To open our hearts to our global family and the community in which God has placed us. Because as we all contribute, we begin to mend the broken relationships that characterize our world.

Reflection

 01 What do you think you have lost, personally, living in an individualistic society?

 02 What concerns do you have about living in a more community-minded way? What risks might be involved?

 03 Jean Vanier connects community with dying to oneself (Luke 9:23-24). With this in mind, why is community so challenging for us?

Action

Invite one of your neighbours over for dinner, or plan a block party with your neighbours' help.

Prayer

Lord, some days my own burdens feel more than heavy enough. I feel weary and even afraid at the thought of letting the concerns of others in. Would You help me to be shaped more by You than by my culture? Help me to open my heart to the community You have placed me in. Amen.

DAY 20 Solidarity

"Do nothing out of selfish ambition or vain conceit. Rather, in humility value others above yourselves, not looking to your own interests but each of you to the interests of the others. In your relationships with one another, have the same mindset as Christ Jesus."

Philippians 2:3-5

"Though the West's efforts through international aid have been well-intentioned, they have often done more harm than good. By focusing on what the poor lack, instead of what they have, the underlying message sent to the poor is this: you are incapable."

– Peter Greer

All of us—even the Son of God—need people to stand with us. As Jesus went to pray in the Garden of Gethsemane, feeling deeply troubled, He asked His disciples to stay with him: "He said to them, 'My soul is overwhelmed with sorrow to the point of death. Stay here and keep watch with me'" (Matthew 26:38).

The word *solidarity* comes from the French and means "mutual responsibility." It means standing with others, stepping into their shoes and then acting as though their needs were our own.

In the first chapter of Isaiah, God tells the Israelites: "Learn to do right; seek justice. Defend the oppressed. Take up the cause of the fatherless; plead the case of the widow" (Isaiah 1:17). God calls us to stand with people in need, adopting their causes as though they are our own. He tells us to "speak up for those who cannot speak for themselves, for the rights of all who are destitute. Speak up and judge fairly; defend the rights of the poor and needy" (Proverbs 31:8-9).

When we ask God to help us see others as He does, we see things in a new way. We start to think about how we would want to be loved if we were the homeless person, the person living on welfare, or the person living in a refugee camp. We begin to identify with people living in poverty and have empathy for them, rather than just sympathy. The barriers between "us" and "them" begin to break down.

We no longer want to do something *for* them, but we start to stand alongside them in solidarity to do something *with* them. People living in poverty are no longer viewed as strangers or a service project, but as our fellow human beings.

Solidarity means that in our response to poverty, we take actions that respect and honour the other person. Here are a few principles that can help us stand in solidarity with those in need. These principles can help you determine how you should respond to issues in your community and help you decide what types of organizations you want to support.

Engage in relationship. North Americans tend to be task oriented, rather than relationship oriented. Our focus can be on getting things done and accomplishing certain goals. But, as broken relationships are at the core of poverty, building relationships in responding to poverty is critical. We need to listen to others, learn from them and build friendships. (If you are ever involved in short-term mission trips, this is vital!)

Drop your agenda. Sometimes we approach a problem thinking we have it all figured out. We have one particular idea in mind, a pet project, that we really want to execute. But we may find that our ideas aren't actually great solutions; they might not actually respond to the root causes of a particular problem. Be humble enough to drop your own agenda and embrace a different vision.

Reduce the power differential. Often, those responding to need are the ones with all the power in the relationship and who make all the decisions. Relinquish power so that you can truly engage in partnership.

Engage in partnership. Do not allow your response to poverty to be one-way, assuming that you are the only one who has something to give. Work to discover what both parties' skills and resources include and allow yourself to receive as well as give.

Acknowledge that everyone has a voice. In the past, aid to people in need was often top-down. Outsiders determined what the solution to the problem was. Ensure that in responding to poverty, everyone has a voice. Those living in the situation know best the context and causes of the problems. Come alongside in helping people solve problems, rather than assuming you have all the answers.

Seek solutions that empower. Together, find solutions to issues that build the capacities of people in need and that allow them to take an active role. Don't do things for people that they are capable of doing themselves.

Seek solutions that get to the root of the problem. Together, determine what the deep issues are that create the problem. Don't offer short-term or short-sighted solutions, but find solutions that will create long-term change. Remember that the root of poverty is spiritual and that through the gospel God can redeem people and situations.

Be committed. Sometimes, we want to be involved in a quick project that makes us feel like we've done good and accomplished something. But real problems are rarely quick and easy fixes. If you truly want to make a difference, be committed to people and relationships for the long haul.

Continually learn. No one gets things right the first time, or the second time for that matter. Be willing to continually learn from one another and make changes as they need to be made.

Pray. Keep your service to God centred on Him so that you can be refreshed and renewed. Ask God to guide your steps and help you correct your missteps.

Standing in solidarity with people in need is not easy. But it is what we are called to. Just as Jesus didn't look to His own interests but to the interests of others (Philippians 2:4), even to the extent of dying for us, He calls us to stand in solidarity with those in need, speaking up for them and standing with them.

Reflection

01 How has your attitude towards people living in poverty or with other needs shifted over the last several weeks?

02 Which item in today's list stood out to you most?

03 Why is it important that we don't approach the poor with an attitude of knowing better or doing for them what they could do?

Action

Reflect on the list. Consider ways in which you have not followed these principles in the past. Pray to God, repent of any negative attitudes, and ask for His guidance.

Prayer

Lord, I appreciate that You stepped into my shoes, that You fully identified with me on the cross. Thank You. Would You help me to move toward a place where I can stand with others in true solidarity? Help me never to treat anyone as a project or a statistic but to recognize their value as a person. Amen.

Seeing the World

BIG PICTURE

We've looked at most of the relationships broken by the Fall—our relationships with God, with ourselves and with others. This week, we will look at the ways our relationship with the world around us is affected by the Fall and by Jesus' redeeming work. It is so easy to focus on having more, doing more, and being more. But God tells us that nothing we have is ours, we are simply stewards of the resources he has given us. This week, we'll explore how God calls us to participate in His mission in the world in our daily living as people who work, consume, and live in relationship with one another.

ADDITIONAL RESOURCES

- Alcorn, Randy. *The Treasure Principle: Unlocking the Secret of Joyful Giving.* Multnomah Books, 2005.

- Blomberg, Craig L. *Neither Poverty Nor Riches: A Biblical Theology of Possessions.* InterVarsity Press, 2006.

Called to Cultivate

"God blessed them and said to them, 'Be fruitful and increase in number; fill the earth and subdue it. Rule over the fish in the sea and the birds in the sky and over every living creature that moves on the ground.'"

Genesis 1:28

"God cares not only about redeeming souls but also about restoring his creation. He calls us to be agents not only of his saving grace but also of his common grace. Our job is not only to build up the church but also to build a society to the glory of God. As agents of God's common grace, we are called to help sustain and renew his creation, to uphold the created institutions of family and society, to pursue science and scholarship, to create works of art and beauty, and to heal and help those suffering from the results of the Fall."

– Charles Colson

A number of the parables Jesus told have to do with servants. Often in the parables, the masters go away, leaving servants in charge of the estate. How the servants act in the absence of their masters varies hugely. Some of the servants take the approach of "when the cat's away, the mice will play." But Jesus is very clear that is not the way He wants His kingdom or world to be run. In Luke 12, after a story contrasting wise and lazy managers, Jesus says, "From everyone who has been given much, much will be demanded; and from the one who has been entrusted with much, much more will be asked." (Luke 12:48)

In our busy and complex lives, it can be easy for us to forget God's original mandate to us in Genesis, to forget that we are managers. The word "rule" in the Genesis passage above has sometimes been taken to mean that we can do whatever we want with the world. But the fact is that we are actually called to be managers rather than owners: we are accountable to God for how we manage the natural world.

In the first chapter of Genesis, we are called to work, multiply, and enjoy what we produce.

The problem, again, is the Fall.

We have talked about how the Fall broke our relationships with God, ourselves, and other human beings. This week we look at the fourth relationship affected by the Fall: our relationship with the created world. In the book of Romans, Paul writes that God's good intentions for how human beings live in relationship with the created world was broken by sin. It left the earth longing for the full restoration of God's Kingdom: "For the creation waits in eager expectation for the children of God to be revealed. For the creation was subjected to frustration, not by its own choice, but by the will of the one who subjected it, in hope that the creation itself will be liberated from its bondage to decay and brought into the freedom and glory of the children of God. We know that the whole creation has been groaning as in the pains of childbirth right up to the present time" (Romans 8:19-22).

Our broken relationship with the created world looks a lot of ways. It is fighting over land claims, or the appropriation of land by one nation or tribe over another. It's an abuse and over-exploitation of natural resources. It's an island of microplastic in the Pacific Ocean twice the size of France. Work, as God indicates in Genesis 3:17, becomes tedious and exhausting rather than life-giving and suited to us. It's a source of anxiety if we don't have enough, or if we believe the lie that we always need more, we become workaholics. We are driven to acquire, to have the latest and greatest, using more and more of the world's resources.

The passage in Romans reminds us that the redemption Jesus brings does not simply restore our relationship with God, but also our relationship with creation itself. Much of that restoration will not happen until Jesus returns, but we are not to abandon our relationship with the created world any more than we would abandon any of the other relationships. Our job as managers is to carry out God's intention for His creation.

One such example can be found in the Thai village of Huay Khom, which used to be surrounded by lush jungle before the trees were cut down, leaving the hills bald. The Mae Yao River, which the villagers had relied upon for drinking, washing, and bathing was polluted and drying up. The fish, which were used by the villagers for food, were disappearing.

Then a small group of young people from Yaowaraat Church decided to make a difference. The "Karen Youth Water Guardians" started a movement to protect the river and forest, in order to improve their own ability to rely on them as resources and preserve them for future generations. When a Compassion child development centre began in the community, a Water Guardians member became the director. Because Compassion cares that its children become good stewards of God's resources and responsible community members, Water Guardian activities were integrated into the centre's sessions. The children work with local elders and leaders to plant and tend trees, build river dams, and build spawning spots for fish in the preserved area of the Mae Yao River. Almost ten years after this project began, the community is seeing the first fruits of its labour. Turtles and fish are starting to reappear, and the trees are growing tall.

In the first chapter of Colossians, we are reminded that in Christ all things were created, that "in Him all things hold together" (v. 17). Through Jesus, God is "reconcil[ing] to himself all things, whether things on earth or things in heaven" (v. 20). As God's redeemed, we are still called to be managers of the resources God has entrusted to us. He has given us a great honour in allowing us to be stewards of His creation, and, as we'll read tomorrow, our treatment of this world has a lot to do with how the poorest among us fare.

Reflection

01 How does the Fall affect our relationship with the created world God left in our care? How do you experience this in your own life?

02 What does Scripture say about the effects of redemption on the created world? Is this a new thought for you?

03 What might it look like to be a good manager of God's creation?

Action

Take a walk in your neighbourhood and bring a garbage bag with you. Pick up whatever trash you find and dispose of it.

Prayer

Lord, You made this world and said that it was very good. You delight in Your creation and long for it to be restored to Your original intention. Help me respond to Your call to be a wise manager of Your creation and show me both what this looks like, and how my actions affect others. Amen.

The Most Vulnerable

"Is it not enough for you to feed on the good pasture? Must you also trample the rest of your pasture with your feet? Is it not enough for you to drink clear water? Must you also muddy the rest with your feet?"

Ezekiel 34:18

"Tragically, the poor are on the front lines when it comes to the harmful impacts of pollution and environmental degradation. In many instances they are the first to suffer and they absorb the brunt of the destructive consequences due to their poverty and vulnerability."

– Ron Sider

In 2010, a 7.0 earthquake rocked Haiti and killed hundreds of thousands of people. The Hotel Montana, a nice hotel where many foreigners stayed, was toppled, leaving hundreds trapped in the rubble. Many resources were deployed to rescue the foreign travelers trapped in the Hotel Montana, whereas many of those living in poverty in Port-au-Prince were left to dig their own crushed relatives out by hand.

Natural disasters, like earthquakes, volcanoes or hurricanes, can devastate a community. But the ones who are the most vulnerable to these disasters are those with the fewest resources. When Typhoon Haiyan flattened cities in the Philippines in 2013, the wealthy had the resources to evacuate early and quickly. But those living in extreme poverty didn't have as many choices. And their homes, primarily made from bamboo, had no chance of surviving a typhoon of that strength.

People living in poverty are the most vulnerable to environmental risks for a lot of reasons.

At one time, if land became unusable for agriculture, people just moved on to new land. Today, with almost all land being "owned", this is not possible in the same way. And land is being affected, especially for the poor. The UN Convention to Combat Desertification notes that 52% of agricultural land in the world is now moderately or severely degraded. For the poor who often rely on rainwater and subsistence farming, this has a significant impact. According to the UN, 80% of the 925 million people going hungry are smallholder farmers and landless poor in rural areas.

Other environmental factors aggravate the lives of those in poverty. They are those at most risk of malaria and other mosquito-borne diseases. In Latin America, nearly one in five people live in slums, as a result of mass migrations to urban areas in search of work. "People living in crowded circumstances, a lack of piped water, and poor sanitation have given rise to the perfect set of conditions for the transmission of mosquito-borne viruses like Zika," said Amy Y. Vittor, Assistant Professor in Medicine at the University of Florida's Emerging Pathogens Institute. In Sub-Saharan Africa, where malaria kills hundreds of thousands of people each year, the poorest people can't afford mosquito repellant or nets, and often they lack the education to take simple steps to prevent mosquito breeding grounds, such as clearing away stagnant water.

Some environmental issues that people face lead to other social issues. For example, girls living in rural areas in the developing world are often responsible to gather water for their families. When there is no safe water available nearby, they may walk several hours a day to gather water. This increases their likelihood of dropping out of school, as they run out of time during the day. Other girls are at risk of sexual abuse when walking alone in isolated areas to gather water.

Some of the suffering of people in poverty comes because of the economic and political activity—or inactivity—of a society. It's stunning to know that many First Nations communities in Canada experience persistent environmental problems that would normally be found only in a developing country: two-thirds of all First Nation communities in Canada have been under at least one drinking water advisory at some time in the last decade, with some communities having undrinkable water for as long as twenty years.

There are other risks to people in poverty. They often live in the most dangerous or vulnerable places. Two-thirds of the world's largest cities are within metres of sea level, with those poorest often living on the coast of many developing nations. Many island nations are at risk of extinction due to rising seas. Most of the population of the Pacific nation of Kiribati, for instance, has moved to one island after the rest of their land disappeared under the ocean. In the Solomon

Islands, several villages have been entirely destroyed by rising seas, and the residents have been forced to relocate.

Much global manufacturing has been moved to developing nations with less strict environmental codes. The rich can choose not to live near polluting factories, but those living in poverty often cannot. Ron Sider observes that the poor suffer from "polluted rivers and toxic wastes that the rich do not want in their backyards."

While some of the environmental risks to people living in poverty are natural, such as natural disasters, others, such as pollution, are manmade. God's question to the Israelites in Ezekiel 34:18 seems pertinent today: "Is it not enough for you to feed on the good pasture? Must you also trample the rest of your pasture with your feet? Is it not enough for you to drink clear water? Must you also muddy the rest with your feet?"

As we read yesterday, we are called to be managers of God's creation. The way we choose to manage this earth has huge implications, especially for those living in poverty. Seeing how closely people in poverty live with the natural environment, we can know that caring for God's creation is an integral part of ensuring the well-being of all people.

Reflection

In what ways can our choices as stewards and managers of God's creation affect those living in extreme poverty?

Why is ignoring the environment while trying to help people in poverty counterproductive?

How can we work to make sure no one falls through the cracks?

Action

Today drink only tap water, and as you do so, give thanks for the luxury of clean water that freely flows from your tap.

Prayer

Lord, I confess that so often I don't even think about the effects of my actions on others. It's complex and unsettling. But at the same time, You call me to see differently and to act differently. I pray that You would help me to live in a way that cares for others and creation and thus brings glory to You. Amen.

DAY 23 *Compassionate Consumption*

"Then [Jesus] said to them, 'Watch out! Be on your guard against all kinds of greed; life does not consist in an abundance of possessions.'"

Luke 12:15

"There is enough in the world for everyone's need, but not for everyone's greed."

– Frank Buchman

There was a time when God's people, the Israelites, were living in the desert after having escaped from slavery in Egypt. When they began to worry about where their food would come from, God did a curious thing: every day, He sent manna—a bread-like substance—that the people could collect and eat. There was enough for each person. However, God's instructions were clear: they were only to take enough for each day and no more. Those who disobeyed soon found themselves with rotting bread.

God's direction to only take enough bread for each day came to the Israelites before even the Ten Commandments, so Christian musician and speaker Shaun Groves refers to it as "God's first law over His children this side of Egypt." It's not surprising: trusting in God was such a difficult principle for the Israelites to learn. And it's a hard principle for us as well.

While God no longer sends literal manna, this principle of trusting God and not taking more than we need runs throughout the Old and New Testament. In Luke 12, Jesus tells the parable of the "rich fool." This man had a good harvest, so he decided to build bigger barns to store his extra grain. Then, he thought, he could take life easy with his provision secure for years to come. "But God said to him, 'You fool! This very night your life will be demanded from you'...This is how it will be with whoever stores up things for themselves but is not rich toward God" (Luke 12:20-21).

Indeed, as Jesus says to introduce this story, "life does not consist in an abundance of possessions" (Luke 12:15).

But if you look at the way North Americans live, we seem to believe the opposite of this principle. We love to spend and shop. Americans spend more annually on garbage bags than 90 of the world's countries spend on everything. Canadians spend more than $6.6 billion annually on their pets—about the same as the GDP for the countries of Togo and Seychelles. In 1975, the average size of a house in Canada was 1,050 square feet. By 2010, new homes were an average of 1,950 square feet.

When Wess Stafford says, "The opposite of poverty is not wealth, the opposite of poverty is enough," he isn't only talking about the poor. He reminds us that as Christians, our goal should be less about acquiring new things and more about living with enough. As Paul writes in Hebrews 13:5, "Keep your lives free from the love of money and be content with what you have, because God has said, 'Never will I leave you; never will I forsake you.'" Again, God is asking us to trust in Him and not our things.

Christians in the Early Church were an example of this. In the Early Church epistle to Diognetus that dates to the second century, the author says, "[Christians] dwell in their own countries, but only as sojourners." When you look at your own life and your purchasing, would someone say of you that you live as a sojourner in this world—as one who is just passing through?

This doesn't mean that we must live as ascetics. But God asks us to be wise and good stewards of our resources. As you consider purchases, ask yourself these three questions:

1. Is this something I should purchase? Before making a purchase, consider a few questions. Is it something I need? Is it something I can use for God's purposes? Is it something I can use to build relationships? It's not wrong to enjoy the abundance God has given us, but we should do it in the context of having given our resources over to God and trusting in Him. We can demonstrate to a watching world that we believe Jesus—that life is not found in an abundance of possessions.

2. Can I buy it second-hand? If your answer to the first question is yes, consider if you can purchase what you need second-hand. By purchasing second-hand items, we can lessen our demand on the earth's resources and the pollution our over-consumption can cause. We can also use the money we save for God's purposes.

3. Can I find an ethical source? If your answer to the second question is no, then try to find an ethical source for your purchases.

This last one is the most difficult because, just as there aren't easy answers to solve poverty, there aren't easy answers to ensure the products we consume are ethically produced.

The first step is to educate yourself. Visit sites such as goodguide.com and betterworldshopper.com to see ratings for companies and products in terms of their impact on the environment and their treatment of workers. Buying locally when possible can help you have a better knowledge of whether the product was ethically produced.

Often, trying to find ethical sources will mean buying more expensive products— which will give you all the more reason to limit your consumption! For example, there is a reason many inexpensive clothes cost as little as they do. Many of the cheaper brands have low ratings in terms of transparency and treatment of workers. When possible, consider buying fewer clothing items that are higher priced, but which are higher quality and from companies you are confident in.

Learn about the environmental impact of the foods you eat. As you learn, ask God what steps He might want you to take in order to be a good steward of the land. Become educated about issues such as child labour and slavery being used to create goods you consume. Make the best choices you can, while standing up and advocating for ethical products. Our purchasing choices can be powerful, and if we collectively demand ethical practices from the companies we buy from, it will make a difference.

Examining our role as consumers challenges us to examine our beliefs about God's provision for us, and for everyone. But it is also an opportunity to live creatively and lovingly in the midst of our everyday lives.

Reflection

 01 What is the equivalent of hoarding manna in your life? How might you live differently, knowing that God does provide for us?

 02 Have you ever looked at your shopping habits as a way of doing justice for people in poverty?

 03 If "the opposite of poverty is not wealth, the opposite of poverty is enough", how does that influence your thoughts, feelings and actions about your own life, and that of others?

Action

Check out goodguide.com, and start educating yourself on the issues of ethical products.

Prayer

Lord, thank You for providing for me and meeting my needs. Please help me to live in a way that helps others have enough too. Help me use creativity and wisdom as a consumer. Amen.

DAY 24 Generosity

"Remember this: Whoever sows sparingly will also reap sparingly, and whoever sows generously will also reap generously. Each of you should give what you have decided in your heart to give, not reluctantly or under compulsion, for God loves a cheerful giver. And God is able to bless you abundantly, so that in all things at all times, having all that you need, you will abound in every good work. As it is written: 'They have freely scattered their gifts to the poor; their righteousness endures forever.'"

2 Corinthians 9:6-9

"We make a living by what we get, but we make a life by what we give."

– Winston Churchill

Psalm 24:1 begins, "The earth is the LORD's, and everything in it, the world, and all who live in it." While this is true for all people, it is something Christians recognize: that all that we have and are—our bodies, our minds, our souls, our abilities, our jobs, our finances, our time, our relationships, and our environment—is a gift from God, and belongs to Him.

Think of the time Jesus was surrounded by a massive—and hungry—crowd. The need was overwhelming to the disciples. Philip said, "It would take more than half a year's wages to buy enough bread for each one to have a bite!" (John 6:7). But one small boy simply gave all he had to Jesus: five small barley loaves and two small fish. After thanking God for it, Jesus distributed this little lunch so that everyone had as much as they wanted. They even had leftovers!

Serving one another with a spirit of generosity is part of mending our broken relationships with God, ourselves, others, and the world. We all move out of the poverty of these broken relationships as we give ourselves and our resources to God. This is another example of God's upside-down Kingdom, of what Jesus meant when He said, "For whoever wants to save their life will lose it, but whoever loses their life for me will save it." (Luke 9:24)

Our giving isn't motivated by guilt or compulsion but out of a confidence that "God is able to bless you abundantly" (2 Corinthians 9:8). Just as God said to Abraham, "I will bless you...and you will be a blessing" (Genesis 12:2), so He entrusts us with gifts, such as money, knowledge and power, to equip us for everything we need to participate in blessing others.

And you don't have to be among the wealthiest to make a big difference. One day, Jesus sat and watched at the temple as the crowd gave their offerings. He saw the rich people give large amounts. But He also watched as a poor widow put in her two small copper coins, which were worth only a few cents. Jesus said, "Truly I tell you, this poor widow has put more into the treasury than all the others. They all gave out of their wealth; but she, out of her poverty, put in everything—all she had to live on." (Mark 12:43-44) Like the widow and the boy with the loaves and fishes, God is able to multiply our offerings to Him to accomplish His purposes.

Lini and Gil Sopoco from St. Thomas, ON, are Compassion sponsors, but it hasn't always been easy. Sometimes they've been between jobs and have had to trust God from payment to payment. Other times, they've needed to suspend their support for a few months while they got back on their feet. But they have still always been faithful to continue giving, even when it was hard. At times when they had a little extra money, they would give small family gifts to their sponsored child, Diana.

They had no idea how God had multiplied their faithfulness and generosity to change Diana and her family's life. Diana's father died due to HIV/AIDS, and her mother was left to support her six children alone. Because of the stigma of this disease, the family became outcasts in their community. Diana's younger sister died from malnutrition during this time because the family didn't have enough to eat. But then something changed: Diana was sponsored by the Sopocos. The Sopocos sent a family gift of $65, and Diana's mom used it to invest in her struggling vegetable business. The Sopocos later sent $90, and Diana's mom was able to expand her business even further. Now, she makes enough from her business to provide the basic necessities for her children and send them to school.

"When I can make a sacrifice; it might seem like a big one at the moment," says Lini. "But when I see how it's changing lives, it's really not."

In thinking about what generosity might look like in your own life, consider 2 Corinthians 8:13-15: "Our desire is not that others might be relieved while you are hard pressed, but that there might be equality. At the present time your plenty will supply what they need, so that in turn their plenty will supply what you need. The goal is equality, as it is written: 'The one who gathered much did not have too much, and the one who gathered little did not have too little.'"

God has given us the mandate to care for others and every resource necessary for the task. He has made us stewards of money, knowledge, talents and a brief amount of time on earth in which to make a difference. When we entrust our resources to God, He is able to use our sacrifices to do big things. The story of the widow reminds us that we don't have to be wealthy to be generous: we simply have to offer all God has given us back to Him in service of others.

Reflection

01 In what ways are you practising generosity with your time, talents, and money?

02 What holds you back from being generous?

03 Review your last few days: where have you seen opportunities to be generous? How did you respond? How might you respond now?

Action

Make a list of the time, talent, and gifts God has entrusted you with. (Think outside the box too: maybe it is a rack of suits you never wear or an ability to cook.) Prayerfully ask God how you can be generous with these gifts and then take a step.

Prayer

Lord, the story of the little boy sharing his lunch and the poor widow giving all she had are humbling to me. Even though I try to be generous, too often I forget that everything is Yours. Help me to live, work and give in a way that blesses others and honours You. Amen.

DAY 25
Everyday Mission

"Then Jesus came to them and said, 'All authority in heaven and on earth has been given to me. Therefore go and make disciples of all nations, baptizing them in the name of the Father and of the Son and of the Holy Spirit, and teaching them to obey everything I have commanded you. And surely I am with you always, to the very end of the age.'"

Matthew 28:18-20

"Every Christian is either a missionary or an imposter."

– Charles H. Spurgeon

Close your eyes and picture a missionary. Do you imagine a super-Christian, called to abandon family, friends and home to "go over there" to a remote and needy part of the globe? In the Great Commission in Matthew 28—Jesus' final instructions to His disciples—the Greek word translated as "go" is literally translated "as you are going." This command is not a calling for the select few to "go on a mission trip" or "go somewhere," but a command for all of us to make disciples as we go along, wherever we may live. That is, God has called each one of us to live out His mission in the place where He has called us.

This isn't just any mission, but one that touches every aspect of our lives. It is an everyday, all-encompassing mission.

In our everyday lives, we are to steward every area of life to accomplish God's mission in the world. We are to see the world God left in our care as a mission field—a place where we compassionately and responsibly steward all that we are, and all that we have to help people flourish physically, socially, economically and spiritually as disciples of Jesus.

This comes back to seeing poverty as a result of broken people in broken relationships. God calls us to respond accordingly, seeking restoration and pursuing wholeness through Jesus. Regardless of what our daily life looks like, God calls us to give people a glimpse of the Kingdom of God by bringing compassion, justice, peace and the good news of Jesus to our neighbours and communities. Just as Jesus "became flesh and made his dwelling among us" (John 1:14), we make our dwelling in our communities, engaging in this everyday, all-encompassing mission.

That's exactly what Karen Reed did. She bought a house in a Vancouver neighbourhood that has often been hostile toward Christianity, and began simply living among her neighbours. Her inspiration was Jeremiah 29:7: "Seek the peace and prosperity of the city...because if it prospers, you too will prosper."

Reed says, "If the church is to be the foretaste of the Kingdom of God, how will people taste that unless we are among them, giving them a glimpse of how we handle conflict, live generously and joyfully?" She adds, "Neighbours aren't projects but people to enjoy, love and invite into our lives. We aren't bringing God into the neighbourhood either, but joining Him where He is already working."

Joining with God and giving others a glimpse of His Kingdom sometimes involves walking and praying in the neighbourhood, organizing a refugee sponsorship, growing food and offering a community kitchen with a regular soup night for the neighbourhood. Reed is living as a missionary right where she is, caring for her neighbours spiritually, physically, socially and economically. "It provides a taste of the Kingdom," says Reed. "People say the whole neighbourhood has changed."

Christians are also at work being everyday missionaries around the world. Ronnie Kaweesa is Compassion Uganda's water expert. Raised in the capital city of Kampala, he took for granted that he could turn on a tap and have water whenever he wanted. Growing up, he was interested in the sciences, and he wanted to find a way to use his gifts to serve God and others. As he began to see that many of his fellow Ugandans, especially in rural areas, did not have safe water or sanitation, Kaweesa decided to dedicate his career to bringing people safe water. He now works with local churches to educate the surrounding community in how to have safe water and sanitation practices. Kaweesa recognizes how caring for people physically is part of our all-encompassing mission as Christians: "All of life is a sacred act of worship, including the [water and sanitation] program. At the end of the day, Compassion is not just providing water; it is providing living water that brings health to the children and their families".

Reed and Kaweesa's lives look very different from each other from the outside. But they are both being everyday missionaries in the way God has called and gifted them. They are both stewarding the resources God has given them to help broken people begin to find wholeness and health.

Some of us are called to go far away while others are called to stay local. But we are all called to participate as missionaries in the place we live. In the daily choices we make to serve and protect others, and in the words we speak that bring truth and light, we are Christ's messengers. We give Him our whole lives— every aspect of them—to benefit His Kingdom. We live as sojourners in this world, using all God has given us to bring Him glory and bring His message of mercy and hope to this world.

Over the last five weeks, we've absorbed a lot of information. We've considered what the spiritual roots of poverty are. We've looked at the four broken relationships that have resulted from the Fall. We've asked God to give us eyes to see what He sees. Now it's time to see the world around us as our mission field.

Reflection

01 — What does it mean to you to engage in a mission that touches all aspects of everyday life?

02 — How might your work, your home and your relationships be places where you could help restore the results of the Fall?

03 — Where do you think people might get a glimpse the Kingdom of God in the way you live?

Action

As you live and work today, remind yourself that you are a missionary— called to participate in an everyday, all-encompassing mission, and to engage with people and work accordingly.

Prayer

Lord, help us to live our lives in a way that gives people a glimpse or a taste of Your Kingdom. Help us make big and small choices to live as missionaries in the places You call us to, whether here or elsewhere. Use my whole life for Your Kingdom. Amen.

Being Jesus to a World In Need

BIG PICTURE

We've spent the last five weeks learning more about poverty and gaining a biblical understanding of how to respond. This week, we'll explore what all of this means for our lives. We'll ask God to use us to reflect the love and light that Jesus offers this world. We'll discuss, pray and commit to take a first step. We'll ask God to guide us as to how He would have us move forward.

ADDITIONAL RESOURCES

- Chan, Francis. *Crazy Love: Overwhelmed by a Relentless God*. David C. Cook Publishing, 2008.

- Voskamp, Ann. *The Broken Way: A Daring Path into the Abundant Life*. Zondervan, 2016.

Created for Such a Time as This

"Then your light will break forth like the dawn, and your healing will quickly appear; then your righteousness will go before you, and the glory of the Lord will be your rear guard. Then you will call, and the Lord will answer; you will cry for help, and he will say: Here am I. If you do away with the yoke of oppression, with the pointing finger and malicious talk, and if you spend yourselves in behalf of the hungry and satisfy the needs of the oppressed, then your light will rise in the darkness, and your night will become like the noonday. The Lord will guide you always; he will satisfy your needs in a sun-scorched land and will strengthen your frame. You will be like a well-watered garden, like a spring whose waters never fail. Your people will rebuild the ancient ruins and will raise up the age-old foundations; you will be called Repairer of Broken Walls, Restorer of Streets with Dwellings."

Isaiah 58:8-12

"God's definition of what matters is pretty straightforward. He measures our lives by how we love."

– Francis Chan

Translation is challenging work. If you've ever used an Internet translation program, you recognize that a direct translation often loses something in the process. Bible translators, in particular, work hard to make sure that the intention of the original language, of God's original message, comes through clearly. Sometimes, looking at how different translators render the same idea helps us better understand what God means.

In the passage above, about halfway through, is a curious little phrase: "if you spend yourselves in behalf of the needy" (Isaiah 58:10). What does it mean to spend yourself? Money comes to mind when we think of spending. But being asked to spend ourselves is something that is more sacrificial than dropping a few coins in a Salvation Army kettle. "Spend yourself" is also translated as "pour yourself out", "give yourself", and "draw out thy soul."

When God tells us to spend ourselves on behalf of the needy, it is not simply a question of meeting needs but doing so with both compassion and all that we are—drawing out our souls and pouring ourselves out for others. God is not simply directing His followers to help others, but to do so with empathy, compassion, affection, and kindness. We are to open wide the doors to the storeroom so that those who are needy can be fully satisfied.

The life of a Christ-follower is one of loving God, loving ourselves, loving each other and loving the world in a way that brings us all to wholeness. It's less about "doing something" and much more about following Christ and becoming more like Him. In John 10, Jesus explains to His followers that He lays His life down: "I am the good shepherd. The good shepherd lays down his life for the sheep." (John 10:11) Later, He calls His followers to do likewise, "For whoever wants to save their life will lose it, but whoever loses their life for me will find it." (Matthew 16:25)

Spending ourselves on behalf of those in need might feel costly—and it is—but it is one of the ways God intends to bring us and all people to wholeness in all of our relationships. God's plan to transform the world involves each of us acting as missionaries whose words, actions, and sacrificial lives bring light, love, hope, and grace to the places God has called us.

The story of Esther in the Old Testament provides an example of someone who recognized that God put her exactly where she was and that He would accomplish his purposes through her actions and words. In a kingdom where the Jewish people are despised, somehow it is Jewish Esther who catches the king's eye and is made his wife. As the threat to the Jewish people rises and they become subject to persecution, Esther's cousin challenges her, saying, "And who knows but that you have come to your royal position for such a time as this?" (Esther 4:14) It is through Esther's brave acceptance of God's call that God saves His people.

Like Esther, God invites each of us to recognize that He has placed us where we are and given us gifts in order to accomplish His purposes of restoring all people in all their relationships in such a time as this.

God invites us to slow down and see the needs around us, to allow God to fill our hearts with compassion—and then to spend ourselves in a way that loves as we would want to be loved. As we would want our child to be loved, as if we were the homeless person, the family living without clean water, the sex trade worker, the person living with addiction. As Francis Chan says, "God's definition of what matters is pretty straightforward. He measures our lives by how we love."

God calls us to spend ourselves on behalf of the needy and the poor. It's a tall order, but He also promises His guidance and provision for all He calls us to: "The Lord will guide you always; he will satisfy your needs in a sun-scorched land and will strengthen your frame. You will be like a well-watered garden, like a spring whose waters never fail." (Isaiah 58:11)

Reflection

 01 "Spending ourselves on the needy feels costly—and it is." What fears does this statement set off in you? How do you (or God) respond to those fears?

 02 What is exciting about the fact that God has placed you somewhere specific, for such a time as this?

 03 Do you already have a sense of what God is calling you to do?

Action

Today, take one action that allows you to spend yourself on behalf of those in need.

Prayer

Lord, I know that You place each of us exactly where You want us, that You call us to see the needs around us and to respond by spending ourselves on their behalf. Help me to see those needs and to be willing to respond in compassionate love. Amen.

DAY 27

The Place God Calls You

"For we are God's handiwork, created in Christ Jesus to do good works, which God prepared in advance for us to do."
Ephesians 2:10

"The place God calls you to is the place where your deep gladness and the world's deep hunger meet."
– Frederick Buechner

If we are ever unsure of God's intimate love for each one of us, the way He designs every aspect of our lives and places us exactly where He wants us to be, we only have to read through Psalm 139. God is not only fully aware of all our activity but He designed us and knew what our lives would look like even before we were born.

It's also clear that God makes use of all our uniqueness to equip us for the specific work he has in mind for us. It's freeing to realize that God doesn't expect us to do everything. We don't have to be the same as another Christian—because in fact, our uniqueness means we can never be exactly like someone else! God's call and the gifts He gives each of us is as different as our individual fingerprints. God knows exactly where He has put us and how He has equipped us. The Bible tells us, "But in fact God has placed the parts in the body, every one of them, just as he wanted them to be." (1 Corinthians 12:18)

At the same time, God has very clear plans for each of us. As Ephesians 2:10 says, he has prepared specific good works in advance for each of us to do! And when we use the way God created us in order to serve Him, we become more like Christ.

So, how do we figure out what that looks like? It is revealed in our gifts, skills, and passions.

Gifts: God gives each Christian "spiritual gifts" in order to serve the Body of Christ and others. Romans 12:6-8, 1 Corinthians 12:7-10 and 12:27-28 as well as Ephesians 4:11 list spiritual gifts God gives to Christians. It's clear that no one receives all the gifts, and no one receives none. Our job is to identify how God has gifted us and to use those gifts in service.

Connect with your church leaders to find out if they have any resources to help you discover your spiritual gifts. Also, pay attention to what others point out in you, or what kinds of ministry you are drawn to. You can also make use of what are called "spiritual gift inventories" (available free online) to help you ask good questions about who God has created you to be in Christ. Pray that God will reveal your gifts, and then simply try serving in the areas you suspect He has gifted you.

Skills: It's easy to see why musical skills are useful to the church, but maybe you haven't really considered how your professional skills, green thumb or sense of humour can be used for God's Kingdom. There are a lot of creative ways you can use your skills to love others. For example, if you love to cook, maybe you could teach a refugee family how to cook using Canadian appliances and food. That's exactly what Grant Memorial Church in Winnipeg, MB, has been doing through its women's ministry group. Think through the various skills you have. Ask God how He might use them for His purposes. You might just be surprised!

Passions: Have you ever noticed that when you listen to the news, some stories break your heart or inspire you while others that are perhaps equally compelling just slide right by? Some things just capture our heart and ignite our passion. Often our passions arise out of our personal experiences—something we've suffered through, a place we've visited, or something that we've just always been intrigued by.

Ask yourself what your passions are. What really gets you revved up and excited? Or what can move you to tears? Are there particular ministries in your church that have always attracted you? Or are there ministries that you've always thought your church ought to have? Ask God for His guidance as you think through what your passions might be.

Chopper Wilson is the director of World Mission at Grant Memorial Church, and part of his job is helping people find where God might be calling them to act. He says, "A lot of times, people overthink this and struggle, not realizing there are just opportunities all around us. Sometimes you don't need to take a massive jump, but being willing to do something for an afternoon may reveal a passion and gift you didn't know you had."

Assess needs: As part of considering the place God has called us to, we also need to assess the needs around us, both locally and globally. As we've learned, we don't simply want to come to problems with our own agendas or preconceived notions already in place. We need to take time to assess the issues and responses before we jump into action.

Find out what the needs in your community and globally are. Find out how people are currently responding to these needs. Consider the responses in light of the root causes of the issues and whether the responses will make a long-term impact. Consider the list on day 20. In what ways can you respond to issues that will allow you to engage in partnership, listen, and learn?

Assessing needs is an ongoing process; you will keep learning as you keep serving. And it does not happen in a vacuum. Engage with other people and learn from their experiences and wisdom.

As we consider where God might be calling us to serve Him, we can trust that He will guide us. The first step is to pray for that guidance. He will show us what He wants us to do and how He has uniquely qualified us to do it.

Reflection

 01 What gifts and skills do you have that you can use to serve others?

 02 What passions has God given you?

 03 What needs do you see in your local community and globally?

Action

Take a spiritual gifts inventory online and talk to trusted church members about what they think your gifts might be.

Prayer

Lord, You made me in all my uniqueness. You placed me where you did for a reason. Help me to see how You have made me and to allow my gifts and gladness to meet the world's need in service. Amen.

Practical Ways to Respond Locally

"Love must be sincere. Hate what is evil; cling to what is good. Be devoted to one another in love. Honor one another above yourselves. Never be lacking in zeal, but keep your spiritual fervor, serving the Lord. Be joyful in hope, patient in affliction, faithful in prayer. Share with the Lord's people who are in need. Practice hospitality. Bless those who persecute you; bless and do not curse. Rejoice with those who rejoice; mourn with those who mourn. Live in harmony with one another. Do not be proud, but be willing to associate with people of low position. Do not be conceited."

Romans 12:9-16

"Faith in action is love, and love in action is service. By transforming that faith into living acts of love, we put ourselves in contact with God Himself, with Jesus our Lord."

– Mother Teresa

We began this journey with the theory that seeing is loving. We said when we really see, we are changed. When we put a face or a name to a story, when we actually see a difference happening, well, that is when our heart starts getting engaged. That is when we get excited and inspired.

So now it's time to roll up our sleeves.

Pray: For those of us who are itching to get into action, for whom seeing has become loving, we might in our hearts feel impatient about starting with prayer. We want to get out there and do something. But as theologian Ole Hallesby writes, "The work of praying is prerequisite to all other work in the kingdom of God, for the simple reason that it is by prayer that we couple the powers of heaven to our helplessness...the powers which can capture strongholds and make the impossible possible."

When we *don't* start with prayer, we can slide too quickly into our own agendas, feeling like we are heroes or saviours. We can too easily cut God out of the equation and follow our own plan. When we pray, we remember our own poverty and our dependence on God. We also recognize that prayer is perhaps the best thing we can do. Because poverty is a spiritual issue with broken relationships at the core, we remember to ask God to be the one who is transforming us and others.

Before you do anything else, pray consistently for God's guidance on how He would have you take action to help others. Pray that God would fill you with His Holy Spirit so that you can remain rooted in Him and depend on His strength while helping others. Pray that God would help His love and mercy overflow out of your life and into the lives of others.

Although it may seem mysterious, we also know that God operates by using our prayers to change the world around us. Ephesians 6:18 tells us, "Pray in the Spirit on all occasions with all kinds of prayers and requests."

Here are some ideas for how you can incorporate prayer into helping others:

- Consider joining your church's prayer ministry
  (or if there isn't one, maybe one should be started!)
- Commit to pray for someone in need at the same time each day
  for a set period of time
- Pray as you walk around your neighbourhood for its specific needs
- Pray as you read the news
- Pray with others for the needs of your community
- Pray for those in authority—government leaders at all levels
  (1 Timothy 2:2)

Live: When we see, we not only love, but we are compelled to do something. God calls us to demonstrate love to others, and especially the poor, marginalized, and needy, in the way we live our lives. We've talked about how the gospel heals both heart and socio-economic issues. These should be deeply tied together in your service. One of the ways to do this is to seek long-term partnerships. This will allow you to get to know people and their stories, and for them to get to know yours—including the love of Jesus.

For Metro Community Church in Kelowna, BC, church is not a weekly event but a daily rhythm of life. In addition to Sunday services, 30 or 40 members of their community, many of whom live on the streets, begin each day together with prayer. Throughout the week, staff and church members together operate a centre that includes a community garden, art studios, music studio, social enterprise businesses, and coffee shop. They also provide counselling and care. They visit people in prison and in the hospital, as well as supervise visits with children and advocate in court.

Here are a few ideas for how we can live differently:

- Advocate for just systems in your community and country with your votes and voice
- When issues arise in your community, stand in solidarity with the marginalized
- Shop locally at stores you know use ethical practices
- If you employ others, pay them a living wage. For example, if your church uses a cleaning service, ensure the employees are compensated fairly.
- Give people in your church who are from marginalized groups a voice at the table
- Engage in relationships with marginalized people in your community—pay attention to their strengths as well as needs, come alongside them in a circle of support
- Become involved in mercy ministries already established in your church
- Consider where there may be gaps in the ministries your church offers
- Get involved with local organizations that are already at work helping needy people in your community. This could include a food bank, ESL classes, support groups for people with disabilities, groups that work with underprivileged children, foster children or street youth.
- Consider if there's a way you can uniquely use your gifts to serve. Start a community garden, provide meals for people, find ways to refresh and bless those who are already helping others, etc.

Give: We've been reminded that all we have and are belongs to God—when we consider how to respond to God's call, this includes our finances. Jesus' story about the servants who were each given money to invest by their master in his absence (Matthew 25:14-30) shows us that God wants us to invest what He has given us—and where more would He want us to invest than in the places and people that reflect His priorities? This parable of the talents condemns the approach of playing it safe—and instead says that God rewards those who make wise investments.

How we can give wisely:

- Give first to your church and the ministries of mercy they already have in place.
- Put your money where your heart is: become a regular donor to local charities that work in areas you are passionate about and that recognize the spiritual roots of poverty by offering the hope of the gospel.
- Raise funds and awareness for local causes that reflect Jesus' Kingdom values.
- Be spontaneous and generous in your giving—and also be wise. Many Christians carry Tim Horton's gift cards and offer them to homeless people, rather than giving away money.

Remember that generous living extends beyond money, and includes other resources. Think through what resources you have that you can use to serve others. You can donate clothing or bedding to a shelter. You could use your vehicle to help a single mom move into an apartment. You could use your home to allow a church member in need to stay with you for a time.

God is in the business of rescuing the world. That's what He did in the death of Jesus on the cross for our salvation. It's also what He's still doing today—drawing people to His grace and at the same time inviting each and every person in the world into an abundant life here and now, and forever. Just as He calls us to love Him with all our heart, soul, mind and strength, so He cares about the well-being not only of people's souls but also hearts, minds and bodies.

Reflection

 How is Jesus calling me to pray specifically for my community?

 How is Jesus calling me to live differently in my community?

 How is Jesus calling me to give wisely in my community?

Action

Pick one of the local suggestions and try it today.

Prayer

Lord, thank You for placing me right where I am. You have blessed me so that I might be a blessing. Help me to see with Your eyes, and then to be Your hands and feet in this place. Amen.

Practical Ways to Respond Globally

"Then the righteous will answer him, 'Lord, when did we see you hungry and feed you? Or thirsty and give you something to drink? When did we see you a stranger and invite you, or needing clothes and clothe you? When did we see you sick or in prison and go to visit you?' The King will reply, 'Truly I tell you, whatever you did for one of the least of these brothers and sisters of mine, you did for me.'"

Matthew 25:37-46

"Sometimes I want to ask God why he allows poverty, famine, and injustice in the world when He could do something about it, but I'm afraid he might just ask me the same question."

– Anonymous

In Matthew 25, Jesus told one of his most startling parables. He says a time will come when the sheep are separated from the goats—those who will receive their inheritance with Christ and those who will be told to depart from Him. And the way His followers are distinguished? They were the ones who gave "the least of these my brothers and sisters" something to drink, showed them hospitality, clothed them, and visited them in their time of need.

We demonstrate our love for Christ whenever we serve anyone who is poor, marginalized or oppressed, including the 12.7 per cent of the world who live on less than $1.90 per day.

But it is perhaps children around the world who are most profoundly affected by the injustice of poverty. Compassion's President Emeritus, Wess Stafford says, "No matter what the ill of society, it tends to spiral downward and eventually land with its cruelest and most smothering impact on our littlest citizens...When hunger and famine strike a nation, adults become weak and hungry but it is the children who most often starve to death. When disease arrives with all its fury, adults can become very sick, but the first to die are usually the children. When war erupts...it is the littlest victims who pay the price...when prostitution reaches its sickest, most depraved form, it becomes child prostitution."

The needs around the world are extensive, but we've learned that God has a plan for how He wants to use each of us specifically. We don't have to respond to every need, but simply to obey His call on our own lives. We've learned that we all experience poverty in a way, and we all have different gifts and skills. We've learned that we ought to engage in partnership with those in need in a way that respects and involves them. We've learned that, at its heart, poverty, is about broken relationships, so it's important to address the root causes of poverty—including hearts and souls. We've learned how the gospel of Christ can transform people and communities and allow them to break free from the cycle of poverty.

So, how do we respond practically to the needs of people around the world?

Pray: Again, it starts with prayer. When we pray for the world, God changes our heart and our lives so that we are "transformed by the renewing of your mind. Then you will be able to test and approve what God's will is—his good, pleasing and perfect will." (Romans 12:2)

How we can pray specifically:

- Bring your fears about the state of the world to God in prayer so that He can fill you with His peace and a sense of His purpose
- Ask God to guide you in knowing where specifically He wants you to engage with the needs of people around the world
- Choose to fast while praying, especially when making specific requests of God or during a time of natural disaster or political crisis
- Receive Compassion's Prayer of the Day email to pray along with the needs of our church partners around the world: https://www.compassion.ca/prayer/
- Use Compassion's resource on how to pray for children: http://www.compassion.com/get-involved/52-ways-to-pray-for-children.htm
- Pray for the persecuted Church: www.persecution.com

Live: As we stand in solidarity with people in need around the world, we recognize that our choices in the way we live have an impact on their lives. We recognize that being a good neighbour to those in need means living our lives in a way that cares for their needs as well as our own.

How we can live differently:

- Find ways for your church to build partnerships with other churches that are located in areas of great need
- Raise awareness of and advocate for issues that are impacting children, such as extreme poverty, child labour and slavery
- Use betterworldshopper.com or slaveryfootprint.org to guide your purchases
- Reward companies with your business when they demonstrate practices that empower people living in poverty
- Take steps to lessen your impact on the environment
- Call on our federal government to focus foreign policy on justice for people in poverty, fairer trade practices, and basic human rights for all

Give: In 2 Corinthians 8, Paul describes generosity as a gift of grace that God gave to the Macedonian church—a church that itself was going through "very severe trials" and yet "gave as much as they were able, and even beyond their ability." This "grace of giving" arises from our hearts when we truly see others as God does.

There are many ways to put our money where our heart is. Ask for God's guidance in where you should give. In light of what we've learned over the past six weeks, here are some ways we can give wisely:

- Donate to organizations that support the work of local churches in the developing world and support the spread of the gospel
- Support organizations that focus on the root causes of poverty, not offering short-term or superficial solutions but long-term change.
- Support organizations that encourage and facilitate community participation to truly transform people
- In times of natural disaster or political turmoil, send donations for relief quickly to make a life-or-death difference
- Support organizations that are fighting injustice that impacts people in poverty, such as International Justice Mission
- Help people in developing countries gain access to vital infrastructure, such as safe water and sanitation. (One way you can do this is through Compassion's Gift Guide: www.compassion.ca/gifts)
- Address the root causes of poverty by helping children develop in all the areas of their lives through Compassion's sponsorship program. www.compassion.ca

Taking everything into mind that we've learned through this series, the most effective way Compassion has found to respond to poverty in the lives of children is holistic child development. That means that we help children in all aspects of their lives—minds, bodies and relationships—while giving them the opportunity to hear the gospel of Jesus Christ and be discipled. Children are given the opportunity to go to school, while also being tutored and mentored at their Compassion centre, to help them make plans for their future. They are given the medical care they need, while also being educated about practices to lead a healthy life. They are given a safe place to learn how to build healthy relationships while learning people skills that will increase their likelihood of employment. They hear the gospel of Christ and can take hold of the hope Christ holds for each one of our lives.

Developing children holistically means that we are responding to the root causes of poverty and breaking the generational cycle of poverty in their lives. Compassion's sponsorship program is run exclusively in partnership with the local church in developing countries, so sponsoring is a way of coming alongside churches and equipping them to respond to the needs in their community.

God, who is aware even of the death of a sparrow and who says that people are worth far more than sparrows (Matthew 10: 29-31), sees the state of our world with compassion. He also invites us to join Him in spending ourselves on behalf of those in need through our prayers, lives and giving.

Reflection

 How is Jesus calling me to pray specifically for needs in this world?

 How is Jesus calling me to live differently in order to benefit His world?

 How is Jesus calling me to give wisely to global needs?

Action

Pick one of the global suggestions above and try it today.

Prayer

Lord, thank You that You are a God of compassion. Thank you for allowing the Church and me to be your hands and feet to bring help to those in need. Help us to do Your will. Amen.

A Journey of Restoration

"They will be his people, and God himself will be with them and be their God. 'He will wipe every tear from their eyes. There will be no more death' or mourning or crying or pain, for the old order of things has passed away.' He who was seated on the throne said, 'I am making everything new!'"

Revelation 21:3-5

"Revelation 21-22 make it clear that the ultimate purpose of redemption is not to escape the material world, but to renew it. God's purpose is not only saving individuals, but also inaugurating a new world based on justice, peace, and love, not power, strife, and selfishness."

— Tim Keller

Something in us craves a happy ending. We want to hear the minor chords resolve into major chords. We are surprised by death and suffering, even when we should be used to it. Something deep inside us whispers that this is not how it should be.

The glorious good news is that a happy ending is on its way.

The Kingdom of God may be like a mustard seed—the smallest of all seeds, as Jesus said, "Yet when planted, it grows and becomes the largest of all garden plants, with such big branches that the birds can perch in its shade." (Mark 4:32)

We only get glimpses of it now because there is still trouble and pain and poverty in the world. We are still broken and poor—all of us—but Jesus has died on the Cross, has been resurrected, and has overcome the world.

Like the shepherd searching for the one lost sheep, or the woman turning her house upside down to find a lost coin, Jesus is finding the lost, restoring them with great rejoicing and putting right all that is wrong with the world.

He invites us, His beloved Bride, the Church, to join Him on His journey of restoration—and in so doing, restores our brokenness along the way. We can rejoice with Him on the way, too, when we see signs of the Kingdom rising up like fresh green shoots in the spring. God says, "See, I am doing a new thing! Now it springs up; do you not perceive it? I am making a way in the wilderness and streams in the wasteland." (Isaiah 43:19)

God also rejoices over us and blesses us as we are faithful in the work He has given us to do and in the place He has put us. As individuals, we are not called to save everyone or respond to every need in the world. God has simply asked us to be faithful with the few things He has placed in our lives. In the parable of the sheep and goats, the master says, "Well done, good and faithful servant! You have been faithful with a few things; I will put you in charge of many things. Come and share your master's happiness!" (Matthew 25:23)

But we're not there yet. We live in a tension between what is and what will be. We see clear signs of hope that God is restoring all things to Himself. We also still clearly see the damage of the Fall in this broken world. But we can rejoice because we know that God is not finished yet.

There will come a day when the picture given to us in the book of Revelation will come true:

> "'Never again will they hunger;
> never again will they thirst.
> The sun will not beat down on them,'
> nor any scorching heat.
> For the Lamb at the center of the throne
> will be their shepherd;
> 'he will lead them to springs of living water.'
> 'And God will wipe away every tear from their eyes.'"
> (Revelation 7:16, 17)

A time will come when God will wipe every tear from our eyes and wipe away the suffering of our world. We wait in great anticipation of that day. And until that time, God is working to restore all things to Him.

God invites us to be part of this journey, to participate in His restoration of the world, to bring the beauty of the gospel to others, to celebrate the signs of His

Kingdom as relationships are restored, and to bring Him glory.

Let's join Him in seeing what He sees, loving what he loves, and bringing His hope to this world.

> Now may the God of peace, who through the blood of the eternal covenant
> brought back from the dead our Lord Jesus, that great Shepherd of the sheep,
> equip you with everything good for doing his will,
> and may he work in us what is pleasing to him,
> through Jesus Christ, to whom be glory for ever and ever.

Amen.

Reflection

01 In Revelations 21:5, God says, "I am making everything new." How has He made you new?

02 How does knowing that God is making everything new change your perspective on helping those in poverty?

03 How is God equipping you to join Him in restoring His Kingdom in this world?

Action

Write down a list of the key things God has taught you over the past six weeks. Then write a list of the actions you're going to take in response.

Prayer

Dear Lord, thank you that a day will come when you will wipe away every tear. We wait in eager anticipation of that day. Until then, I offer myself to You as your servant. Please give me eyes to see what You see and heal my heart, so I can respond as you would. Please use me to bring your hope and healing to this world. Amen.

Acknowledgements

Eyes to See is a reality because of the earnest efforts of so many, including

The talented team at Graf-Martin Communications, who brought this resource to life with creativity and insight.

Amber Van Schooneveld, whose passion and pursuit of excellence meant reviewing, editing and re-writing to make this content shine.

The long list of partners and friends that humbly shared their stories and perspectives behind the scenes or on camera.

All the pastors, thought leaders, and Compassion staff who reviewed this resource, gave feedback, and took this content to the next level in its ability to impact the Church in Canada.

Shaun Groves, who said yes to the challenge of hosting a film series and did so with a contagious passion for children, the Church and the gospel.

Tommy Alley at The Inspire Collective, who masterfully captured the beauty and brokenness in our world while producing the *Eyes to See* films.

Allison Alley, National Advocacy Manager, who dreamt up and drove this project forward with vision and conviction.

Barry Slauenwhite, President and CEO, whose leadership and longstanding commitment to mobilize the Church at home and around the world created an environment where these efforts could be realized

More From Compassion

Inspired? We're so glad you've been on this journey with us. To dive deeper and see real-life stories captured from around the globe, don't forget to visit www.eyestosee.ca.

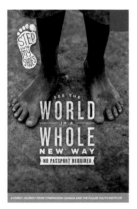

Step into My Shoes is a seven-step immersive experience and devotional for families and groups. In each step, children will walk in the shoes of Ugandan Pastor Tom and his family. They will explore the life of Jesus and see how Scripture calls us to care for those in need. Each step includes a video, devotional, memory verse and hands-on activity. Children will develop a heart of compassion, gratitude and service— all while growing closer to Christ.

Learn more and download the experience for free at www.stepintomyshoes.ca.

True Story: What God Wants Us To Do About Poverty is a six-week curriculum designed to help teens discover their role in God's story of restoring the world. Students will journey alongside Alyssa, a teen from Toronto, and explore the spiritual nature of poverty, God's heart for those in need and the unique role of the Church. Students will be drawn closer to Christ as they discover the difference they can make in the world—and the difference they can help others make as well.

Learn more and download the curriculum for free at www.truestoryseries.ca.

About Compassion

As one of the world's leading child development organizations, Compassion partners with the local church in 25 countries to end poverty in the lives of children and their families. Today, almost two million children and their families are discovering lives full of promise and purpose as they develop in all aspects of their lives—minds, bodies and relationships—while discovering God's love for them in the gospel of Jesus Christ.

Sponsoring a child with Compassion is one of the most effective ways to respond to God's call to reflect His love to a world in need. Recent independent research has shown us what we have known for more than 50 years: Compassion's child development model works! Children across the globe are stepping out of poverty and into lives filled with hope and opportunity—and Compassion sponsors get to be part of seeing this transformation happen.

To learn more and to sponsor a child, visit www.compassion.ca.